MW01680628

TRUE SUCCESS

SHEILA FEJERAN

TRUE SUCCESS

MASTER YOUR MIND, YOUR HEART, YOUR ACTIONS AND CREATE YOUR LIFE

AFFIRMATION + AFFORMATION + PRAYER = HAVING A "MIRACLE" MORNING EVERY DAY

A Fejeran Books publication.

Contact details www.fejeranbooks.com
P.O. Box 552 Van Alstyne, TX 75495

Scripture quotations marked:
ESV are taken from the English Standard Version.
NASB are taken from the New American Standard Bible.
NLT are taken from the New Living Translation.
NKJV are taken from the New King James Version.
BSB are taken from the Berean Study Bible.

Internet addresses (websites, blogs, etc.) printed in this book are offered as a resource to you. These are not intended in any way to be or imply an endorsement on the part of the author, nor do we vouch for the content of these sites and numbers for the life of this book.

Cover design: PixelStudio
Editor: Janelle Lim

ISBN-13: 978-0692843659 (Fejeran Books)
ISBN-10: 0692843655

DEDICATION

To my mother, Barb Daly, who has single-handedly been the most powerful person in my life. Your love was strong, steady and faithful. You were my rock. Your belief in me and constant encouragement gave me confidence as a young girl. You told me I could be anything I wanted to be. You were always there, cheering me on and building me up. You instilled in me a determination and focus that cannot be bought. For that I am eternally grateful. You are the whisper in my ear saying I can do it!

To my young men, Garrett and Jordan, who were my gifts from God when I was told I could not have children. I came to understand the love of God because of my intense love for you. My love for you overwhelms me. I am so very grateful I get to be your mom, so thankful to be in your lives and so very proud of the men you are becoming. I am most proud to see the love and convictions you are developing in your own walk with the Lord.

To Emily Nicholson, you taught me what it means to love Jesus. You taught me how to go on dates with God and have special times with Him, to make my relationship with Him real. You taught me how to pour myself out for other people and how to become a living sacrifice.

To Leigh Kinnard, you are an amazing example of Jesus, in your own love, sacrifice, heart and convictions. You give your time, energy and everything you have to other people. Your intense love for your children is what inspired me when I had my boys. Your joy and laughter is contagious and I will treasure the memories of the time we served together in New York.

Karene Goff, who is my soul sister. We share so many of

the same struggles and strengths. I believe God has continuously brought us into each other's lives when we needed each other most. I'm so very grateful to be called your friend.

Gordon Ferguson, who is my adopted dad in the faith. You were my hope when I didn't have any, leading me through the storm. As an author, over the years you have been my inspiration through the words you have penned on behalf of Christ and have powerfully impacted my life. My gratitude to you is eternal and my thankfulness beyond words.

To my coaches Brian Dobbs, Hoss Pratt and Matt Graham who helped me face my fears, conquer my obstacles and determine my destiny. You have had a profound impact on my mindset and on my business.

To Chandler Bolt and the Self Publishing School, who gave me the training and support to make this happen. This has been one of the most rewarding investments.

To Janelle Lim, PixelStudio and Ankit Pradhan, who helped bring all of this together through their brilliance in editing, illustration and formatting.

Every word of this book is devoted to God, my Father; to Jesus, who is my best friend, my living and only hope, for His glory and prayerfully for your edification; and to the Holy Spirit, who gives me the power to become everything I was intended to be.

CONTENTS

<u>CONTENTS</u>

INTRODUCTION

In today's world, many people are searching for True Success. They want answers on how to achieve their dreams, overcome situations in their lives and have the life they truly desire. Some people are desperate for a change, willing to do whatever it takes to achieve the life they are looking for. It doesn't matter if you want to grow spiritually, become more financially successful, have a better marriage or overcome personal struggles. There is a way and an answer on how to change.

Throughout the years, there have been tactics and routines successful entrepreneurs have used to become massively wealthy. Many times you hear very successful people talk about what happened that launched them to greatness. Normally each one has a story about what was a game changer for them. It could have been a book they read, a mentor that came into their life or a devastating situation they went through. Each of them came face to face with where they were at in life and what it was going to take to get to where they really wanted to be. I have realized that many people do not take the time to train themselves to be successful, to be more than conquerors. It is time to take hold of those principles and apply it to every area of our lives.

True Success takes a look at the skills and knowledge of successful business people, who have obtained wealth, alongside the calling and heart of Jesus, who has already won the victory.

As a professional sales trainer and a Christian for over 25 years, I have been trained and taught how to succeed in the corporate world. I have had successful careers in the media, pharmaceutical and real estate industries. Being coached by some of the top trainers in the country has given me an insight and blueprint on how to become successful. It has given me the power to overcome in every area of my life. In this book, I bring together the blueprint for success in business and introduce those techniques in the context of being a Christian who overcomes and glorifies God. Many of the people I have worked with have gained incredible success by following the principles I am going to share with you in this book. The best part is you can start putting these principles into practice today and start achieving results. Through helping people, I finally came to the conviction and conclusion that I needed to share this information.

I promise that if you put into practice the ideas and actions in this book, it will change your life. You will find you have become so much more than you ever dreamed you could be and are accomplishing more than you ever imagined. Every area of your life from your marriage, struggles, finances, health and mental well being can drastically change for the better if you put these practices into action.

Don't wait until it is too late. Don't live with regret. Take the time to find out what simple steps you can take to change your life. We are all just one piece of information away from greatness. As they say, you don't know what you don't know. Books give us the avenue to expand our knowledge, change our understanding, and provide us the pieces to change our lives.

The principles of this book have proven over and over to create a complete transformation in the lives of those who take hold and take action! Everything you need to become the best version of you is at your fingertips. Each chapter walks you through steps that will transform each area of your life. Take control of your life! Make it happen! Create the life of your dreams

PERSPECTIVE

What does true success mean to you? Each one of us has a different definition of success. Some of us want to be a Hollywood star, some of us want to be millionaires or billionaires, some of us want to be parents, and some of us want to be missionaries.

We all maintain perspective or reference point that gives us our definition. It comes from how we were raised, people who impacted us along the way, or even a dream; but, each of us forms opinions and perspectives based on that past acceptance of information and knowledge that we store in our conscious and subconscious. Part of being successful is defining what you believe success to be, evaluating your perspectives and opinions. The other part is determining what you need to do to get there.

Over the years, I have had the opportunity to work with and associate with many millionaires and very successful people, what we call Game Changers. Many of them have overcome extreme situations to get to where they are. Many of them have achieved what most people classify as success because they have a lot of money, a big house, exotic cars and all of the things the world has to offer.

What I have noticed is that in spite of all they have, there is something missing for many of them. A very successful national coach in our industry committed suicide this past year. He had the world at his fingertips, but he made a choice that it wasn't enough. When you listen to what

Steve Jobs had to say at the end of his life, talking about regret for not going after the things that really mattered. You realize he was so focused on getting the stuff that he missed out on the true treasure.

My goal is to make sure you don't miss the mark, that you won't get to the end of your life and say, "I Wish…." I want you to be able to live a life of intention, decision and passion. I want you to be able to overcome any obstacle and achieve greatness in your life for your own benefit as well as the benefit of all of the lives you will touch.
So, to those of you who are already very successful and have accomplished everything you want, this book is really about bringing you in line with what it is going to take to gain true success, not just things.

Over the years, I have seen many people controlled by their struggles and circumstances. They are not experiencing the victorious life, full life offered to them. Some of you are struggling with having success or becoming successful. Others of you seem to be on a vicious cycle of failure, negativity and not being able to overcome the internal battles going on in their head as well as the external circumstances that keep them from becoming what you consider to be successful. This book is to help you step up and get out of the cycles of the past and become the conquerors that you were intended to be in order to have the promised life you desire.

As far as my perspective, I am operating from a Christian philosophy and belief that believes the Bible is the Word of

God and Jesus is the Son of God who came to earth, lived and died for our sins and is seated at the right hand of God. I believe that God provides His Holy Spirit as a Counselor until the day Christ returns. I will be sharing many scriptures on topics throughout this book, which will give you an organized, focused way to tackle some of the bigger issues you may be going through.

It is important to understand that what I am describing to you in the following text is not magic or something superstitious. I will be explaining to you how the discovery of science, psychology, neuroscience, history and spirituality all come together. This creates the most powerful force known to man in order to achieve the greatest success possible.

Psalm 1:1-3 (NIV) says:

> Blessed is the man who walks not in the counsel of the wicked, nor stands in the way of sinners, nor sits in the seat of scoffers; but his delight is in the law of the Lord, and on his law he meditates day and night. He is like a tree planted by streams of water that yields its fruit in its season, and its leaf does not wither. In all that he does, he prospers.

I. POWER OF WORDS

1. PUT YOUR MONEY WHERE YOUR MOUTH IS

If you have ever taken the time to think about it, everything we do revolves around words. Our language, communication, relationships, celebrations and congratulations all revolve around words. Many times being successful includes a powerful use of words and command of your native language. There are countless books, seminars and workshops available to teach you how to use words to get what you want, negotiate deals and make yourself look a certain way. There are self-help books, history books, science books and more all filled with words that teach and expand our minds as they describe a specific topic.

One of my first experiences with the power of words was in college, which was a long time ago. I was in a speech communications course and did a study on the power of words from the book, "Word Play: What Happens When People Talk," by Peter Farb (1993). I remember being completely enamored by the book. Up until that point in my life, I was not what you would consider a voracious reader. I read what I had to in order to get by, but it was not what I would call a passion. This was a turning point for me in my career and my life. Obviously, since a book on words is what has ignited my passion all of these years, my hope is that through my explanation of the power of words you will be inspired to use them to transform your life as well.

Before we get into the meat of the content, I want you to

really understand the power of words. This will play a huge role when we get to the practical aspects of putting it all together. Let's look at where words come from and how it all started.

Genesis 1:1-3 says, "In the beginning God created the heavens and the earth. Now the earth was formless and empty, darkness was over the surface of the deep, and the Spirit of God was hovering over the waters. And God said, 'Let there be light,' and there was light."

Did you get that? From the very beginning God used words to bring everything into existence. As you continue reading, God spoke sky, land, vegetation, morning, evening, creatures in the water and air, and creatures on land as well as man into being! Wow, if that doesn't show you how powerful words can be, I don't know what will.

Sorry ladies, I didn't forget about us. God did say in Genesis 2:18, "It is not good for the man to be alone. I will make a helper suitable for him." God did not speak us into existence. Genesis 2:22 says, "Then the Lord God made a woman from the rib he had taken out of the man." I say God decided to take His time making us because we were the last and the crowning glory of His creation.

A sobering and sad part to the power of words is in Genesis 3:1:

> Now the serpent was more crafty than any of the wild animals the Lord God had made. He <u>said</u> to the woman, "'Did God really <u>say</u>, 'You must not eat from

any tree in the garden?'"

The rest, as they say, was history. The woman ate the fruit, the woman gave some to the man, both of their eyes were opened and they saw their nakedness. God walked in the garden and they hid from Him, God called them out on what they did, the man blamed the woman and the woman blamed the serpent. It was too late. Their eyes were opened. They were deceived. The doubt was planted, the pride and desire of wanting to be like God was exposed. The beginning of what has plagued man for all of history began – we blame someone else for what we do.

Just to give a little encouragement to the startling plight and truth of where words have gotten us is in John 1:1-4:

> In the beginning was the Word (Jesus), and the Word (Jesus) was with God, and the Word (Jesus) was God. He (Jesus) was with God in the beginning. Through Him (Jesus) all things were made; without Him (Jesus) nothing was made that has been made. In Him (Jesus) was life, and that life was the light of men.

God knew us, He knew what we would do, He knew our hearts and He already had the answer. It is amazing that God calls Jesus the Word. God is saying Jesus is the answer, Jesus is the power; in Jesus is life and Jesus is the light of men.

In Revelation, it describes the rider on a white horse and Jesus coming in the end. Chapter 19:13 says, "He is dressed in a robe dipped in blood, and his name is the Word of God."

Hebrews 4:12 says, "The word of God is alive and active. Sharper than any double-edged sword, it penetrates even to dividing soul and spirit, joints and marrow; it judges the thoughts and attitudes of the heart."

John 15:7 says, "If you remain in me and my words remain in you, ask whatever you wish, and it will be done for you."

When you read the Bible, you are not just reading a book made from paper and trees. You are reading the living and breathing Word. When we need answers to our questions, help with our struggles and saving from our circumstances, we need to get into the Word that breathes life into us through its pages. Breathe it in; take it in. Like incense or sweet smelling food, breathe deep and take in the Word of God. It will give you life. It will answer your questions.

You may have heard people say, "Put your money where your mouth is." This phrase reinforces the idea that you have to back up your words with actions, which is what I am going to help you do through the information provided. We are going to give you the information you need to become a person known for their word and worth their weight in gold.

As you can see, words are powerful, life changing and life creating. Words can be used to create a beginning and end. They have a power and energy that we send out when we speak them. They go out into the world to order, command, dictate and bring about circumstances and consequences. Now that we know where words come from and the power of their existence, let's talk about the power of using them together to bring about an end result.

2. <u>I AM</u>

"I AM - Two of the most powerful words. For what you put after them shapes your reality." – Unknown

The first time we hear the exchange of these words together is in Exodus 3:14 when God is communicating with Moses about who He is. Moses wants to figure out how to describe God to the Israelites he is supposed to help free:

> God said to Moses, "I AM WHO I AM. This is what you are to say to the Israelites: 'I AM has sent me to you.'"

I grew up watching Popeye. I have to admit the first time I read that scripture, that famous spinach-eating sailor flashed through mind, saying, "I am what I am." Although Popeye was a supernatural being when he ate his spinach, notice that he said "what" instead of "who." Popeye changed "what" he was. He became super strong and able to beat Brutus up to impress his sweetie. God, on the other hand, describes "who" He is. He is "I Am."

Have you ever thought about that when you say I am this or I am that? Since God is I AM, whenever you say "I Am" you are actually stepping into His presence. You are comparing yourself with His authority, standing in His place, pretending to have His power. That may seem a little much, but think about it. I am going to go to school, I am going to marry them, and I am going to take that job. If you really think about it, you are saying something that you really don't know, really can't dictate and really don't have the true power to say. You could drop dead in your tracks at just that moment. On the way to the appointment, a bus could hit you. So when I make statements and say "I am," really I am calling on God to step up to the plate and answer my request, take care of working that situation out or bless me with what just came off of my lips. I am saying that I am calling on the author of the universe to lend me His ear, His power, His glory.

The Bible makes it very clear for us in James 4:13, which says:

> Now listen, you who say, "Today or tomorrow we will go to this or that city, spend a year there, carry on business and make money." Why, you do not even know what will happen tomorrow. What is your life? You are a mist that appears for a little while and then vanishes.

Now, let's turn it around for a minute. Am I going to go to school, am I going to get that job, am I going to do this or that? When we switch the words around it gives us a completely different perspective and understanding. It changes our focus from an authority to a submissive or questioning position. I am bringing this up because this will be important later when you consider the words you use, the way you arrange them and the authority you attach to them.

There is a song that comes to mind when I think about *I Am*. Rhema Marvanne (2011) wrote "Just As I am" when she was eight years old. It is about coming just as I am and is a powerfully moving explanation and example of what we are really like in our minds if we will be honest about it (Marvanne, 2011).

"Just As I Am"

Dear Lord,
I'm on my knees again
I come to you, because You understand

I've tried so hard
But I just can't change myself
That's why I know I need Your help

So here I am
This is my plea
My only hope
Is Your love for me

I'm reaching out
So desperately
Come take my hand,
Take all of me
JUST AS I AM

Oh Lord,
You make what's broken new
Why can't I, just learn to follow You

I wanna know you
To feel you in my soul
I surrender all control

So here I am
This is my plea
My only hope
Is Your love for me

I'm reaching out
So desperately
Come take my hand,
Take all of me
JUST AS I AM Not afraid
To follow You, where You lead me

I can leave the past behind me
I'm forgiven and I'm free
So here I am---
My only hope
Is Your love for me
I'm reaching out
So desperately

Come take my hand,
Take all of me
JUST AS I AM---

Oh
Your love for me
I'm reaching out

So desperately
Come take my hand,
Take all of me
Just as
I Am (Marvanne, 2011, Believe)

An inspiring film, produced by Tom Shadyac in 2011 and titled, "I Am," grapples with questions about life that Shadyac himself asked after making his own major lifestyle changes ("I Am: The Film"). Despite grossing nearly two billion dollars with his films and possessing things like a 17,000 square foot art-filled mansion, he says, "What I discovered, when I looked deeply, was that the world I was living in was a lie," adding, "Much to my surprise, the accumulation of material wealth was a neutral phenomenon, neither good or bad, and certainly did not buy happiness" ("I Am: The Film," 2011). Based on this reevaluation of life and what he considered important, he sold all of his possessions and settled for a much simpler existence, which led him to ask himself some important questions, "If this is for me—if I really am going to die—what do I want to say before I go? What will be my last testament?" ("I Am: The Film," 2011). Determining life was more than the things one possesses; it is understandable Shadyac would begin asking introspective questions. Shadyac states, "…The solution begins with a deeper transformation that must occur in each of us. I AM isn't as much about what you can do, as who you can be. And from that transformation of being, action will naturally follow," and, thus, "I Am" was born ("I Am: The Film," 2011).

That last statement is the most important one. Who can you be? Stop worrying about keeping up with the Jones' or having more than your neighbors. Stop looking at things of this world and start looking at the people in this world.
I love the movement, "I Am Second." It has spread around the world and, globally, has inspired and changed people. When we understand we are part of something greater and live for something beyond ourselves, we can invite change, create opportunity and alter destiny.

What are you going to use your words to accomplish? What course are you going to chart for your life? What are you going to focus on and achieve to make a lasting impact on this world?

3. STICKS AND STONES

Needless to say, when The Christian Recorder of March 1862 presented as an old adage "Sticks and stones will break my bones, but words will never harm me," I guess they hadn't taken the time to really think about what words actually do (Martin, 2012). Words are actually one of the most powerful forces on earth. They created the earth. Words have the power to destroy or inspire life. They start wars and lead people to take their lives, but they also heal hearts and demonstrate love.

Have you ever had anyone say to you that their word is their bond? We put a lot of stock in people's words and their meanings. Based on words, we decide if we are going to trust people, be their friends, marry them or never talk to them again. Everyone, whether they say it or not, will judge you on your words. Your words can curse, encourage, heal or sooth.

Because of my love for words, I have utter indignation when someone doesn't keep their word. My word is my bond. I am relentless about keeping my word. If I tell you I am going to do something, it is as good as gold. I go so far that when I realize I am not going to be able to fulfill my word for some reason, I call you and tell you that I am not going to be able to do it and why.

There is a scripture I think about often, especially when dealing with a difficult situation, that assists me in handling myself the right way. It is in 1 Peter 4:11, which says, "If anyone speaks, they should do so as one who speaks the very words of God." I think that is a pretty concise way of spelling it out. It has been said that words are x-rays of the heart!

One of the most important decisions I made in my life was how my children would be raised. The single biggest decision I made was how my children would be spoken to. I knew I did not want to repeat history. I did not want my children to go through and deal with the destruction of their life and character simply because things were said to them that aimed to define who they are.

The first decision I made was a commitment to never tell the boys they were bad. I decided that we were going to separate "who" the boys were from "what" they did. We were going to make sure everything we said was positive, loving, encouraging, motivating and inspiring. We worked to build our boys up to know they were gifts and that we prayed for them and about them. We wanted them to know they were our treasured possessions and we were blessed to be their parents. I was determined they would have self-confidence and security in knowing they were loved, wanted and cherished.

For those of you with children, especially older children, you are thinking, "Right, like you really did that with your children." My boys are now 15 and 17 and they will tell you that I never once said they were bad or said negative things about them. Now that does not mean I have not dealt with their character. We read many books on how to discipline children and sought a lot of advice from friends, family and church members. But even when I was most angry, I never became vengeful or lashed out at them with my tongue. I would absolutely punish them, take things away and talk to them strongly about how their actions were completely unacceptable. I would not accept that behavior, and they had to make a choice and bear the consequences of those choices. I did this when they were really young as well. As soon as they started walking, I would talk with them and, if they kept up, I would take things away.

One of my favorite shows that came out many years later was "Supernanny." It starred a British nanny who was brilliant with children. They sent her into the worst situations to clean up the mess families had become due to unruly children.

That was really the same way I raised my boys. When they would do something that was wrong or bad, we would stop and have a conversation. I would tell them that what they were doing was unacceptable and that they needed to change their behavior. I let them know they had a choice to make. They could continue doing what they were doing, knowing the consequences that would result from that decision, or they could change their behavior. I can tell you, that although we had many temper tantrums in the beginning of setting those boundaries, the boys quickly learned that having their favorite toy taken away or having to sit by themselves and not being able to play was not fun. It wasn't too long before my boys would quickly make the choice to stop doing what was considered unacceptable behavior and start doing what was right.

What I learned is that I didn't have to spank my kids, my children made choices of their own free will and did the right thing. They learned how to "self-manage" their emotions, how to decipher good from bad choices and that there are consequences to every choice they make. They can either have positive results from making the right choices or they can have negative consequences from making unacceptable choices.

Over the years, all I had to do was tell the boys I was going to count to three and by the time I reached two they would usually stop whatever they were doing. They knew if I hit three they were not going to like what happened next. The key was that I would actually do what I said. If I told them I was going to take a toy away, I would do it. If I said they could not go out with their friends, I didn't let them. Every single time, no matter how painful it was, I followed through with whatever the consequence was. Through that consistency and follow through, my boys knew exactly what was coming if they made the choice to continue in their actions.

When you make a decision about something for your own life, you begin to notice a running theme with those around you. It was shocking to me to see how people treated their children, even in public places. I have heard people screaming at their children, cussing at them, dragging them through stores or hitting them. It breaks my heart when I see news reports of child abuse or children being killed by their parents.

For each person who makes the decision to become a parent, they have the power and authority given to them to determine how they will speak to their children and what they will do to build them up and not tear them down. From my experience, it is a whole lot harder to succeed when you have to overcome mountains from your childhood before you have entered the race.

Sticks and stone may break your bones but words can always hurt you. One of the first steps of change is to determine the words coming out of your mouth that you speak to others, as well as the words you speak to yourself. You are going to build up, not tear down. Your words are going to inspire others, fire them up and fuel the flame of faith. Determine to master your words and be a master of your words.

4. WORDS ARE CURRENCY

One of the primary ghostwriters for many CEO's and superstars is Tammy Kling. She coined a phrase when she was speaking at a conference I was attending that has become a mantra for her: "Words are currency" (Kling, 2014). What a great way to describe words.

I would like to conduct a little experiment with you. I am going to list a string of words together. I want you to read each word out loud in a slow methodical voice and visualize each word in your mind. Are you ready? Okay, here we go:

Truth, Love, Peace, Joy, Lord, Master, Savior, Friend, Infinite, Almighty, Invincible, Indescribable, King, Healer, Holy, Hope, Character, Uncontainable.

Did you feel how powerful the effects of just one word can be and then how overwhelmingly powerful a string of words can be together? One of the most powerful messages and masterful use of words was by Dr. S. M. Lockridge (1976) in "That's My King, Do You Know Him?" It is available for viewing on YouTube and is worth your time.

One of my earliest memories as a child was a desire to become a television news anchor. I wanted to be the next Barbara Walters. I was mesmerized by her style, respect and persuasion. She had a way of finding out things that other people could never pull out of someone. I never waivered on my desire and went into college studying radio, television and film.

I was able to do a summer internship at a local television station in Cincinnati. Much to my dismay, I quickly realized I wasn't going to be able to fulfill my lifelong dream. I can still remember the scene as the television truck pulled up to the next story. I wasn't sure where we were going or what we were going to cover, but when we got out of the truck and started walking towards the pool area, there was an odd quietness from everyone in the area. There were people whispering amongst themselves, but it wasn't the lively and exciting scenes I had grown used to. As we approached the area, I saw the lifeless body of a little boy they had pulled from the bottom of the pool. No one had covered him up yet and the stark reality of my future life flashed through my mind. I am not sure why I had never thought out it before. Maybe I was so focused on all of the years of watching the news and Barbara Walters that I hadn't really thought about what I was going to be reporting on. I was focused on being a reporter. My dream died that day. As we drove away, I knew I would not be able to handle covering death, dying and all the horrible things people do to each other. I have a very weak stomach and can't even watch the nurse when she takes my blood at the doctor's office.

During my internship, I had numerous conversations with reporters and saw what they went through during the course of the day. They were treated really badly wherever they went. They also spent a lot of time writing and coming up with the content of their stories. Again, I had never really thought about a journalist needing to be a good writer. At that point I did not like writing, except poetry, and really believed I wasn't good at it. I was focused on the public speaking part of being a journalist and using my words and language to tell the story. I thought, "How in the world am I going to be a journalist when I'm not a good writer?" At that point, I hadn't really grappled with the "why" of what was motivating me to be a reporter. In retrospect, I realize it was because I loved the way words were used to tell a story, convey information and move people to act. Not realizing what my true passion was, I decided to go into the radio end of the business. It was being enrolled in a speech communication course that sparked the fire in me. It clicked with me that it was the spoken word that was lighting the fire in me, and it created a new passion in me. I made the decision I was going to finish up my degree in RTF, but I added a second degree in Speech Communication so I could become a lawyer for radio stations. I went full force in the study of speech, language, psychology and persuasion.

As I look back, I wish I had someone that would have been able to help me really figure out what I wanted to do, someone that could have helped me uncover what it was I was passionate about. During my senior year, one of my teachers worked for the most popular radio station in the city. He said it would be a shame for me to go straight to law school because I would be perfect in the radio business. He said I should work for a radio station and see what it is like so I could better understand the business before attending law school. I did a summer internship that went really well and he talked me into doing another internship at the local R&B station.

It was a crazy time. I was taking 21 hours of coursework to finish up my degrees while working for the radio station. I wound up falling in love with the business and they were so impressed with my work that they hired me as a full-time employee when I finished my internship. I was in the sales department and selling ads/radio commercials to sponsors for the station. I was particularly drawn to a specialty in the business, working with large corporations and creating marketing campaigns, which involved bringing companies together to create sweepstakes giveaways, vacations and more. After having quick success, I was recruited within six months and moved to Philadelphia to manage a sales staff, teaching them to do the same kinds of programs.

In many forms, words are currency. In advertising we use them to motivate and persuade people to buy the products of our sponsors. In psychology, they are used to help people delve into and heal from past abuses and damage. Through books, words inspire and inform someone to motivate them to change their lives. Their minds are opened and their hearts are filled by the words of authors. Words are currency. The key for us is we have to make sure we spend them wisely.

5. <u>OUT OF THE MOUTH</u>

Many people do not take the time to stop and think about what comes out of their mouths. They are fueled by anger, arrogance, selfishness or greed. They are self-driven to stand their ground, prove their point or not be embarrassed. If you haven't figured it out by now, I am trying to make a clear distinction about words and how we need to consider very carefully how we use them in every area of our lives as well as with ourselves. The following are several quotes and scriptures I hope you will adopt and receive deep convictions about using in a way that will build up, encourage and inspire.

"False words are not only evil in themselves but they infect the soul with evil." – Plato

"Wise men speak because they have something to say; fools because they have to say something." – Plato

"We have two ears and one mouth so that we can listen twice as much as we speak." – Epictetus

"Kind words can be short and easy to speak, but their echoes are truly endless."– Mother Teresa

"Words can inspire. And words can destroy. Choose yours well." – Robin Sharma

"In the end, we will remember not the words of our enemies, but the silence of our friends."

– Martin Luther King Jr.

“A good man brings good things out of the good stored up in his heart, and an evil man brings evil things out of the evil stored up in his heart. For the mouth speaks what the heart is full of.” – Luke 6:45

“They sharpen their tongues like swords and aim cruel words like deadly arrows.” – Psalm 64:3

“Those who guard their lips preserve their lives, but those who speak rashly will come to ruin.” – Proverbs 13:3

“But no human being can tame the tongue. It is a restless evil, full of deadly poison.”– James 3:8

“The words of the reckless pierce like swords, but the tongue of the wise brings healing.” – Proverbs 12:18

“All you need to say is simply 'Yes' or 'No'; anything beyond this comes from the evil one.” – Matthew 5:37

“Out of the same mouth come praise and cursing. My brothers and sisters, this should not be.” – James 3:10

“I tell you, on the day of judgment people will give account for every careless word they speak.” – Matthew 12:36 (ESV)

“May these words of my mouth and this meditation of my heart be pleasing in your sight, LORD, my Rock and my

Redeemer." – Psalm 19:14 (NIV)

"But now you must also rid yourselves of all such things as these: anger, rage, malice, slander, and filthy language from your lips." – Colossians 3:8

"For by your words you will be acquitted, and by your words you will be condemned." – Matthew 12:37

"Do not let any unwholesome talk come out of your mouths, but only what is helpful for building others up according to their needs, that it may benefit those who listen." – Ephesians 4:29

"Those who consider themselves religious and yet do not keep a tight rein on their tongues deceive themselves, and their religion is worthless." – James 1:26

God cares very much about the words you speak. Everything that comes out of our mouths should not differ from what God would say in that situation. Ouch! That is convicting. I cannot say I do this all the time, but I can tell you that I have very deep convictions about the words I use. We have all blown it with our words, especially in marriages when we get mad at each other. But, you have a choice about what comes out of your mouth. No one makes you say anything. You choose.

I have put a lot of scriptures in here because it speaks for itself. God is very specific about what should come out of our mouths, which ultimately is coming out of our hearts.

Think about whether you are negative, critical, cynical, hateful, vengeful, nasty or foul-mouthed. We also have to think about the impact we want to make on the people around us.

Not only do we have to be careful about what we say to other people. We have to be careful about what we say to ourselves. As you can, words are very powerful. The words you speak to yourself are just as damaging, judgmental and destructive as the words you speak to others, if not more, since you are saying them to vent your feelings. In other translations of Luke 6:45, it says, "For the mouth speaks what the heart is full of." You can tell what someone is like by his or her words. So if you are speaking negatively, critically or cynically, you have to realize that you are speaking what is in your heart. If that is the case, you need to take note and start evaluating it in order to change it.

On another note, we have to remember that whether we are aware of it, or realize it, people judge us as well as our character on whether our words match our actions. No one wants to be in a relationship with someone who talks and talks and talks about what they are going to do when their actions display something very different. We wind up not trusting them and ultimately don't want to have a relationship with them. We want to have great relationships, so we have to be people whose words and actions are cohesive. God wants that too! What do we want to be remembered for?

II. AT THE HEART OF THE MATTER

1. DESPERATE

Desperate – feeling, showing, or involving a hopeless sense that a situation is so bad as to be impossible to deal with; critical, acute, serious risky, final, last-ditch, last-gasp, do-or-die (*Google,* n.d.).

Have you ever felt desperate? After reading the definition, it definitely causes you to pause. When we think about becoming successful, having a better marriage, making more money and growing in relationship with God, we don't normally think about the word *desperate*. We think of words like success, wealth, victory, conqueror or champion. No one likes to think about negative things. No one likes to deal with negative things. When we think of being desperate, it brings about a negative connotation in our minds. When you hear some of the greatest victories or greatest stories of achievement, many of them have their roots in desperateness. It is like an army having their back up against a wall about to be slaughtered if they don't fight or a man who is going to lose his house and everything they own if their financial situation doesn't turn around. When we have great stress and great need in our lives, it produces a focus, energy and we throw caution to the wind mentality we don't operate in on a normal basis.

To begin with, so that you understand where I am coming from, I want to share a parable with you from the Bible that paints a very clear picture of what being desperate entails. There are many ways we can be desperate, but we are going to look at one of the ways.

The Parable of the Lost Son - Luke 15:11-32:

Jesus continued: "There was a man who had two sons. The younger one said to his father, 'Father, give me my share of the estate.' So he divided his property between them.

"Not long after that, the younger son got together all he had, set off for a distant country and there squandered his wealth in wild living. After he had spent everything, there was a severe famine in that whole country, and he began to be in need. So he went and hired himself out to a citizen of that country, who sent him to his fields to feed pigs. He longed to fill his stomach with the pods that the pigs were eating, but no one gave him anything. "When he came to his senses, he said, 'How many of my father's hired servants have food to spare, and here I am starving to death! I will set out and go back to my father and say to him: Father, I have sinned against heaven and against you. I am no longer worthy to be called your son; make me like one of your hired servants.' So he got up and went to his father.

"But while he was still a long way off, his father saw him and was filled with compassion for him; he ran to his son, threw his arms around him and kissed him.

“The son said to him, ‘Father, I have sinned against heaven and against you. I am no longer worthy to be called your son.’

“But the father said to his servants, ‘Quick! Bring the best robe and put it on him. Put a ring on his finger and sandals on his feet. Bring the fattened calf and kill it. Let’s have a feast and celebrate. For this son of mine was dead and is alive again; he was lost and is found.’ So they began to celebrate.

“Meanwhile, the older son was in the field. When he came near the house, he heard music and dancing. So he called one of the servants and asked him what was going on. ‘Your brother has come,’ he replied, ‘and your father has killed the fattened calf because he has him back safe and sound.’

“The older brother became angry and refused to go in. So his father went out and pleaded with him. But he answered his father, ‘Look! All these years I’ve been slaving for you and never disobeyed your orders. Yet you never gave me even a young goat so I could celebrate with my friends. But when this son of yours who has squandered your property with prostitutes comes home, you kill the fattened calf for him!’

“‘My son,’ the father said, ‘you are always with me, and everything I have is yours. But we had to celebrate and be glad, because this brother of yours was dead and is alive again; he was lost and is found.’”

What do you see in this parable? Things had gotten so bad for this guy that he longed to eat the pig's food and he was Jewish. That is a huge issue since the Jews did not eat any part of the pig, not to mention the thought of eating the pig's food would have been the ultimate in humiliation. Have you ever been that low?

I heard a story once about Sylvester Stallone before he became famous. They said he was a starving actor in New York and had been down on his luck. Things got so bad that he lost his marriage and was getting ready to lose his apartment and be on the streets. On the last day he went out and sold his beloved dog to someone for $50. That night he went to a bar with a friend of his and was talking about what was going on, when a boxing match appeared on the television. It was the underdog that was going after the champ and blowing all predictions of what would happen in the fight. He was inspired and spent the next week or two in the library researching and writing the script for Rocky. He would not back down to the studios when they didn't want him to act in it. He held his ground and found someone to produce it. The rest is history.

When we are desperate, we are hungry. We are focused, determined and willing to do anything. We don't care how we look, what other people think and are willing to make total fools of ourselves just to get the object of our desire. There is nothing that matters more; we are sold out for our goal, going for it with everything we have.

You are probably asking yourself, what in the world is she talking about being desperate for? I just want to make more money at work or have a better marriage. Well, the reason I am talking about it is because this is where change begins. If there isn't something that drives you to be sold out, totally committed, or gives you a whatever-it-takes attitude, then change won't last. You will make surface changes but they won't be deep within your soul. The reason why is it involves the heart. In order for us to really change, we have to engage our hearts, not just our minds.

There are many new studies out about the power of the heart. Doctors are now calling it the "little mind" because of the new understanding they have about how it works not just from a functional perspective but from an energy and power perspective. The heart is where all of the blood for all of the organs in the body pumps through. Everything about whether you are alive or dead is based on your heart pumping. It is, if I am not speaking out of turn, the most vital organ in your body. When your heart stops beating, it is over.

The fire that desperation lights in us comes from our heart. It drives us to do crazy things, impossible things and outlandish things to accomplish our goals. Mark my words; you will know when you meet someone who has desperateness about them. You will see it in their eyes; you will hear it in their voice. It isn't a shrink back and cower-in-the-corner type of attitude. It isn't a hide-behind-something and wait-for-someone-to-rescue-you attitude. It is a no-holds-barred passion you can see in them.

You have to get that fire in you, a desperateness that focuses you on your goal, whatever that may be. This fire is going to be what drives you through the next steps. That fire is going to be what cannot be deterred, squelched or extinguished by the distractions or obstacles that come in the way of our goals. That fire gives you what you need to not give up, not change course, turn around or quit. It is what will be the “burning” part of the burning desire that will fan the flames of our desire.

2. DESIRE

Desire – a strong feeling of wanting to have something or wishing for something to happen (*Google*, n.d.).

If desire is where your dreams, hopes and wishes start, we need to focus in on how to harness those desires to become what we choose to be.

In Napoleon Hill's (2000) ground-breaking work that took 25 years of research, "Think and Grow Rich" describes how desire is the number one component for all of the successful people he interviewed. He explains how it can't be a plain desire and a burning desire deep within you that dominates your mindset (Hill, 2000). This is where the desperateness that we just talked about comes in to play. It needs to be an obsession, focus, vision, passion, definite goal and pulsating intensity in you that you are consumed by. You have to be willing to put all your energy, time, resources and will power towards obtaining that desire and goal. A burning desire is the starting point to achievement (Hill, 2000). Along with that desire was a definiteness of purpose that drove them toward their desire. He actually uses the example of Jesus and the definiteness of purpose He possessed (Hill, 2000).

Obviously, there are desires that are good and desires that are not. We need to dig deep to figure out what we really desire. When I described that this book can be a catapult to help you change your life, this is where it starts. We have to become very clear about the good desires we want to go after. In Psalm 37:4, it says, 'Take delight in the Lord, and he will give you the desires of your heart."

We also have to become very clear about how to overcome the bad desires that may have been controlling us up until this point.

In James 1:14, it says, "But each person is tempted when they are dragged away by their own evil desire and enticed."

Another more bold example is in Genesis 4:7, where God is talking to Cain and says, "If you do what is right, will you not be accepted? But if you do not do what is right, sin is crouching at your door; it desires to have you, but you must rule over it."

It will come down to us being able to master our desires, so that we can be ignited by the burning desire to achieve the life that we want and master the desires in us that we have chosen to give up or stop doing.

I imagine this scripture makes things clearer. There are many times I have been in conversations with people and they have described a scene almost identical to this. They talk about feeling like they are being dragged down into the pit of despair, being washed away with overwhelming feelings. I'm sure no one wants to feel this way, so we have to deal with the desires in us that are not good, that are going to take us to places we really don't want to go.

In order to produce change or create anything, you have to begin with a firm foundation, something solid that won't move or break. What I am going to describe is a step-by-step process you will go through in order to get to your ultimate goals. This will take time and is not an overnight, quick fix success system. This is a time honored, time tested process.

One of my favorite books that make clear the importance of this time-honored system is Aesop's Fable, "The Tortoise and the Hare " (Gibbs, 2002, fable 237). This book hits home for me since I have been both. Over the first half of my life, I operated from the system of the hare, running through life, fast paced, not slowing down, not considering the opponent, not focused on the finish line. This last half of my life has been living like the Tortoise, slow and steady, focused on one step at a time, focused on the finish line, not worried about the race anyone else is running, not letting others deter me from my goals. Since you already know who wins the race, I am sure you can guess which part of my life has been the most successful.

Remember, these are building blocks, each one fitting together to build the tower, each one with its own purpose and reason for being part of the structure to ultimately build the desired results.

Discover Desires

"The only man who succeeds is the man who progressively realizes a worthy ideal." – Earl Nightingale

In order to figure all of this out, we have to take time to write out all of the things we desire. Remember that we want to really go after our burning desires. What are you passionate about? What fires you up? What do you love? Find a place that is quiet, where you won't be interrupted. Set aside a few hours to be alone. You can write it out like a letter, you can write it out with bullet points or even randomly all over the page with bubbles circling each topic you write. But, the key is to start writing down everything you desire. You want it to be free flowing, not holding back on ideas or feelings. This process is just the beginning and may take several sessions to get everything out on paper and written out in detail the way you want it to be. You have to be totally honest in the process. Make sure you are writing the desires you want to change. You are going to have to tackle them as well, so you have to be honest about what you are feeling.

Your topics may include wanting to lose weight and get in shape, changing your marriage, stopping smoking, getting a new job, obtaining a degree or changing your relationship with God. It doesn't matter how crazy it may seem or even how impossible. It is very important that you take time to write down everything that comes to mind or you feel is coming from your heart. You can call this "Your Wildest Dreams and Desires List." Don't worry about how you are going to accomplish them; we just want all of your dreams, ideas, desires and wants out on paper.

This is a process called mind mapping, which is very effective. It is taking the time to write down all of the ideas, dreams, visions, desires, wants or needs you can think of. Hill (2000) discusses how dreams are not born of indifference, laziness or a lack of ambition.

Once you have everything out on paper you can think of, we want to organize them into categories in case some of them fall under the same topic. For example, I may list that I want a better marriage, but then I may write that I want to have dates once a week or start praying with my spouse. Take the time to put them into categories by topics with the main headings being things like: marriage, body/health, work, God/spiritual health, friendship, children, personal development and finances. You can make up the main headings for any topics or ideas you have.

Once you have the topics organized by category and each of the ideas you wrote listed under those topics, then you have to take the time to think through each topic. You have to really wrestle with what your goal or burning desire is for the topic. Write out what you want in regards to this topic. It may be a sentence or it may be a paragraph, but the key is to get as specific as possible about that topic and what you would want if you could have it exactly the way you want it. Think through what the outcome would be once you reach what you are wanting. Again, don't worry about how you are going to get there. We are working on putting together the dream first. We will deal with the reality of getting there in a bit.

For example, you may want to lose weight. Your desire is to be at a healthy weight so you will not be made fun of or get discouraging looks from other people. You can describe how you want to feel comfortable in your clothes, even stating the size and the weight you want to be when you are done. You can describe what you would look like and how it would feel when you reach your goal. You have to fix your mind on exactly where you want to be and what it is going to be like when you get there.

The last part of this section is figuring out when you want to get there. One of the main reasons goals are not met is there is not a time frame or a specific deadline. There is something in our brain that kicks in when we know we have a deadline to meet. We can feel a charge of energy running through our body when we get in that fight-or-flight mode of being under the gun and having to complete something. This is an important step; so take the time to think about when you want to set the deadline. Think about timelines that are realistic. You don't want to set yourself up for failure by insisting you are going to lose 30 pounds in two weeks. Realistically, you could lose up to two pounds per week. If you have 30 pounds to lose, then you are looking at a minimum of 15 weeks, or up to 30 weeks, to hit your goal. You will want to do this for each area of your life.

Faith The Facts

What you may have put down on your list of desires may be things that seem so outlandish to you and so out-of-the-box that you can not imagine any way possible that they are going to happen. As we discussed before, we have to have a firm foundation. The two key components to having a foundation are desire and belief. These two mixed together will give you a rock solid and concrete foundation that will be immovable and unshakable. This part may take you more time to wrestle through or contemplate.

Before we begin diving into this topic, let's regress for a moment. We are going to dig deep here, since this is one of the most importance topics for us to cover. Faith is the glue that holds everything else together. So, sit back and take your time to take in all of the information in this section. You may have to read it through a few times since it can be a little intense, but it is very important to immerse yourself in what is being discussed.

As I mentioned earlier, I have been a trainer for over 25 years. While completing my final semester of college, I was working full-time at a radio station and focusing on what they called the "co-op vendor" part of the business. This basically meant I would bring vendors together, like Coca-Cola and Toyota, and create promotions or marketing programs that would advertise their business as well as provide a benefit or giveaway to the public. Within six months, I was recruited, promoted and relocated to Philadelphia to run a sales department of a local radio station and train agents on how to do what I was doing. After a number of years, and a few stations, I moved on to the advertising end of the business for a number of years. Next, I was recruited into the pharmaceutical industry and worked to build a company from \$1 million to \$30 million. Over the years, I recruited, hired, trained and developed the sales staff and created an inside sales staff in two other specialties. After we sold the company, I entered the real estate industry, and quickly brought the training and experience from my previous work with me to build a very successful team and business. Over the last 13 years, I have trained not only the agents in my company, but I serve as a trainer for the DFW market and as a certified trainer for the state of Texas.

The reason I am mentioning all of that is not to puff myself up but to let you know that I have worked in three very different industries as a professional trainer. I have had the best training offered in each of these industries which taught me how to be successful. It also has given me the opportunity to work with many different types of people. I have learned how to develop and train sales people, how to best work with the public as clients and teach and inform them on industry information. This has crystalized for me the different learning styles and personalities of people, which produces the need to make sure the information I am presenting is clear, concise, organized, systematic and methodical in approach. As a trainer, I have to look at the big picture of the information I need to present, break each topic down in bite-size chunks. Lastly, I have to make sure each of the points under each topic will cover the important facts as well as explain the information in a way that can be processed by each learning style of those I train. I want to use these same techniques to help each of you by taking bite-sized bits of information and building them together to create the big picture.

Coincidentally, while spending those 25 years learning and training during my workday, I spent my personal hours learning and training in the scriptures. My mornings were spent scouring the scriptures to gain understanding. I would study books of the Bible, chapters, topics, definitions of words, history and theological writing. I spent my evenings and weekends studying the Bible with women who were interested in learning more about God and the Bible. With any free time I had, I would spend time with those women who had their focus on living out the Bible. Throughout the years, I have been blessed to work side-by-side with some of the greatest leaders and to sit at their feet and learn the wisdom of the scriptures.

It is important to understand that God gave us a brain we are supposed to use. We have to realize God gave us knowledge, wisdom and understanding in many areas of study to help us understand Him more, draw closer to Him, be more in awe of Him and be advocates for Him. I am not in any way trying to replace or put other things before God. I'm working to use and take advantage of all of the knowledge available to us to step up and use it as a platform to bring me into a greater understanding and awe of God.

We will be using some of the most successful techniques from business studies, each representing a building block to build the system we are now discussing. We will then add in the teaching and power from the scriptures to pull it all together. I will describe each technique from my research and what gems I pulled from their system and philosophies.

I must mention that these studies and the work of all these gentlemen are held in high regard. I have studied and practiced everything in each of their books, along with numerous other works on this topic. I would be remiss if I did not recommend reading each of their works to gain a greater understanding and insight into what we are discussing. Each of their works produced in me revelation and enlightenment. As mentioned, each were building blocks, adding to my knowledge and the conclusions we are discussing, not to take away from or diminish the impact of their work in its own right.

I began with the information from Napoleon Hill and the concepts and conclusions that took him 25 years to produce. To date, this is the most comprehensive work by anyone on the topic of success. Hill worked with the likes of Carnegie, Ford, Edison, Schwab, Roosevelt, Rockefeller, Woolworth and many more. Hill's work still transforms the business and lives of many of the most successful people in business today. Hill's work was the framework for success that I started with and built upon. While I will be discussing Hill's (2000) work throughout this book, in regards to the belief and faith part we are currently discussing, he says you have to convince yourself, you have to visualize it happening. He talks about believing the attainment of your desire (Hill, 2000).

Next was "The Miracle Morning: The Not-So Obvious Secret Guaranteed to Transform Your Life" by Hal Elrod (2014). Robert Kiyosaki, #1 bestselling author of "Rich Dad Poor Dad," says, "Hal Elrod is a genius and his book

The Miracle Morning has been magical in my life. What Hal has done is taken the 'best practices'—developed over centuries of human consciousness development—and condensed the 'best of the best; into a daily morning ritual. A ritual that is now part of my day" ("Amazon Review: Hal Elrod's 'The Miracle Morning,'" n.d.).

"The Miracle Morning" process gave feet to my fire. Disciplining myself to wake at 4 a.m. and spending the first few hours of my day completely focused on setting my mind to accomplish whatever it was I desired was an enormous breakthrough for me. Results started immediately in my mind and then, not long after, in my actions. This was a tipping point for me to develop the discipline and structure I needed to work towards greatness. The primary focus of this work for me came from discipline, affirmation and visualization.

Next was one of my favorite books, "The Strangest Secret" by Earl Nightingale (2006). Nightingale says, "A success is anyone who is doing deliberately a pre-determined job, because that's what he decided to do – deliberately" (Nightingale, 2006, p. 9).

He tells us, "The key to success and – the key to failure: We become what we think about" (Nightingale, 2006, p. 13).

Nightingale (2006) describes reaping, sowing and planting in your mind the seeds of what you want to be. He says:

> Now the human mind is far more fertile, far more incredible and mysterious than the land, but it works the same way. It doesn't care what we plant – success, failure; a concrete, worthwhile goal, or confusion, misunderstanding, fear, anxiety and so on. But what we plant, it will return to us. (Nightingale, 2006, p. 22)

Realizing that I can plant into my mind the seeds I want to sow. This work was a light bulb moment realizing how I have to choose and decide what I want to think.

After that came "The Slight Edge: Secret to a Successful Life" by Jeff Olson (2013). This work impacted me because it applied philosophy along with everything else I had learned. As well, this work supported Hill's (2000) theory on desire with the "one thing" being what you focus on. This work fanned the flame burning inside me from previous discoveries.

Next was "Strategic Acceleration: Succeed at the Speed of Life" by Tony Jeary (2009). The building block from this work drove me to gain clarity about my purpose (Jeary 2009), reiterating what Hill (2000) said about Definiteness of Purpose. This was acting as the cement between my blocks, holding them together. Jeary (2009) says, "Our belief window is shaped by the facts or ideas we accept as truth and our personal experience as it relates to those facts" (p. 13).

Lastly was "The Book of Afformations: Discovering the Missing Piece to Abundant Health, Wealth, Love and

Happiness" by Noah St. John (2013). This was where I had a true defining moment. St. John (2013) describes the "Belief Gap," which is the chasm between what you are saying out loud in an affirmation and what you really believe in your heart and mind. An additional point from his work is using questions to ignite the neurolinguistic pathways to change what your subconscious believes (St. John, 2013). This bridges the gap or gets your mind on board with what your mouth was saying, along with what you want to achieve (St. John, 2013). Specifically, he taught that when you begin a question with "Why?" your mind goes into overdrive and searches for an answer (St. John, 2013). It was during the practice and implementation of his work that I had the break-through for this new pathway for achievement.

St. John's work was so impactful to me because of my conviction about the scriptures. As you search through many of the stories and parables in the New Testament, you will see that normally Jesus used questions as a way to communicate information and get other people to think about and figure out what they were doing. He used questions during the first encounter we read about when He was a teenager in the temple. They were in awe of the questions He asked. In the Jewish culture, your wisdom was not revealed by how much information you could tell but by how intuitive the questions were that you asked. They were in awe because the questions Jesus asked astonished them and displayed wisdom far beyond His years. This is very powerful since we can use the same technique by asking the question "Why?" to bring clarity and understanding to our situations.

The next piece of the puzzle started during my studies in Speech Communication. There had been recent breakthroughs in studies of neurolinguistics and the effect on the Reticular Activating System (RAS). While I did not connect the dots at the time, it all came back after reading St. John's (2013) work. Moruzzi and Magoun discovered the RAS in 1949 while studying sleep-wake mechanisms (Steriade, 1996). This system is part of the reticular formation that extends from the brain stem to the midbrain and thalamus, with connections distributed throughout the cerebral cortex that controls the degree of activity of the central nervous system. It plays a role in many important functions, including sleep and waking, behavioral motivation, breathing, and the beating of the heart. The system is used to take information from the conscious to the subconscious brain. Perhaps the most important function of the RAS is its control of consciousness with the ability to consciously focus attention on something. Our minds are constantly bombarded by massive amounts of information, which is received by our senses (visual, auditory, taste, smell and touch). This system allows us to filter the information so we are not on complete information overload.

This is extremely important information in order to assist in having access to the power to focus on what we want. In other words, whatever a person focuses on consciously will manifest subconsciously. We have to be careful what we think about because it will become us. This is an incredible awareness for those of us wanting to change the way we think or live. We have the power built into us, through RAS, to literally create the life we choose. We have to understand our brain only has the capacity to focus on what is in the conscious mind, which is limited. However, the capacity of the unconscious mind is unlimited.

"Getting Things Done: The Art of Stress-Free Productivity," by David Allen (2003), discusses how the RAS works:

> When you focus on something—the vacation you're going to take, the meeting you're about to go into, the project you want to launch--that focus instantly creates ideas and thought patterns you wouldn't have had otherwise. Even your physiology will respond to an image in your head as if it were reality." Allen goes on to describe our brain like a computer, whatever we focus on we identify with. (Allen, 2003, p. 159)

For example, if you decide you want to buy a red truck because your brain is focusing on that red truck, you will feel that every other vehicle you see is a red truck. Your brain has focused on a red truck, so it draws attention and focuses on every other red truck on the road. When you think about it, the same principle applies to other things in our lives such as success, money, love and happiness. If you are not focusing on them, they disappear from your unconscious mind. Like the red truck, they have always been there but they are just unseen. What happens is your beliefs, actions and values all act as filters in your RAS.

By setting goals, you can set your RAS filters. What we will do is take all of the good things you want in your life, focus on them so that your RAS will channel them from your conscious to your subconscious mind and eventually turn them into reality. For the information that your conscious is not currently using or focused on, it will be stored in your subconscious.

Dr. Maxwell Maltz says:

> Your automatic creative mechanism is teleological. That is, it operates in terms of goals and end results. Once you give it a definite goal, to achieve, you can depend upon its automatic guidance system to take you to that goal much better than 'you' ever could by conscious thought. "You" supply the goal by thinking in terms of end results. Your automatic mechanism then supplies the means whereby. (Inspirational Quotes: Maxwell Maltz, n.d.)

Now that you understand a little bit about how the brain works to deliver the thought process, let's talk about putting the beginning of this process together. Since we realize we need to send the correct information we want from our conscious to our subconscious minds, with a focus on what we want to accomplish, Hill's (2000) description as having the purpose or intent set on what our goals are makes sense. We can take that intent, focus, or goal and encourage our subconscious mind to bring a desired goal into reality. We will talk more about focus in a future chapter but we need to understand the power of how we set goals, use words to focus our minds and, ultimately, be able to change.

To put all of these systems together and by adding each building block, it looks something like this:

Hill's desire – I want to… lose 20 pounds.
Eldrod's affirmation/visualization – I will.. lose 20 pounds.
Nightingale's thoughts – I think about and decide.. I will lose 20 pounds.
Olson's philosophy – I believe I can.. lose 20 pounds.
Jeary's clarity – I will.. lose 20 pounds by December 31, 2016.
St. John's use of questions: Why am I having such success losing weight and meeting my goal of losing 20-pounds by the end of the year?

The point of each of their systems is to intentionally: a) create a focus on the desired result; b) put it in writing, which increases your chance of success by 50%; c) set dates to accomplish the goal, which increases likelihood of success; d) read it aloud, which solidifies it in your mind and gives your RAS the ability to convince yourself that you are going to accomplish the goal; and e) actually do something about it – eat right, exercise and work towards the goal.

The word *intent* is derived from the word intend, which means to direct the mind and proceed on course towards a goal. The word *intent* was the Latin *intendere*, which means to stretch towards (*Dictionary.com*, n.d.). We have to stretch our minds and direct our minds towards the goal we have a burning desire to accomplish. You will push your RAS into gear when you expect something to happen; there is movement and action involved. When you set your mind to intentionally accomplish something, you are bringing together the burning desire and definiteness of purpose that Hill (2000) described, along with the clarity that Jeary (2009) describes.

"The thing always happens that you really believe in, and the belief in a thing makes it happen." – Frank Lloyd Wright

"Whatever the mind can conceive and believe, it can achieve." – Napoleon Hill

"Somehow I can't believe that there are any heights that can't be scaled by a man who knows the secrets of making dreams come true. This special secret – curiosity, confidence, courage and constancy, and the greatest of all is confidence. When you believe in a thing, believe in it all the way, implicitly and unquestionable." – Walt Disney

Now that you have a solid understanding of the supporting information, let's pull together how faith or belief comes into play. Faith is confidence or trust in a person or thing (*Dictionary.com*, n.d.). Hill (2000) describes faith as a state of mind, which may be induced, or created, by affirmation or repeated instructions to the subconscious mind, through the principles of auto-suggestion (p. 100). St. John (2006) deals not with the definition but the difference between your current perceived reality and your new desired reality. As with most self-help books or programs that deal with this topic, they use this definition of faith as the bridge for you, along with the use of auto-suggestion, to obtain belief. This is where Hill ended his studies on the topic. All studies from these gentlemen have been proven over and over by the success of millions of people who have put their work into practice. There is no question about their success and the brilliance of their work.

For those of us who profess a faith in Christ, we see faith in a different way. We describe faith as being sure of what we hope for and certain of what we do not see (Heb. 11:1). Faith celebrates and thanks God for things before they happen.

For many people, faith is hard because people often focus on what they have to do to build up their faith. They are told they need to have faith in God but struggle because they aren't really sure how to do that. When I started thinking about the different definitions of faith between the two groups of people, I realized that faith has a lot to do with what you focus on.

If your focus is on getting rich, believing that you are going to get rich, having a burning desire and maintaining a definiteness of purpose towards that goal while making an effort, you will more than likely reach your goal. If you have all of those same components working with your focus on being closer to God and having a focus on Jesus, you will find accomplishing that goal effortless. We will talk more about focus later, but it is a key component to keeping you zeroed in on your goal, whatever it may be. The point being, if we profess a faith in God, then we believe we have access not only to all of the tools and abilities we have talked about but access to what God will bring to the table on our behalf as well.

There are two main scriptures I think of when talking about faith. The first is Romans 10:17, "Consequently, faith comes from hearing the message, and the message is heard through the word about Christ." The second comes from Hebrews 12:2, which says, "Fix your eyes on Jesus, the author and perfecter of our faith." Based on these scriptures, I know that faith comes from the message about Christ, which is in the Bible. If I am not reading the Bible, I am not learning or growing in my faith. Second, if I keep my focus on Jesus, fix my eyes on Him, I will realize He is the author, creator and composer of my faith. He is the one that will give me faith to begin. Next, He is the perfecter of my faith, who will mature, complete, develop and finish my faith. That is an incredible concept. Since having the belief in something is what is going to help you achieve it, we have the ability to super-charge our ability to change, overcome and succeed because of where our faith lies.

With that in mind, for this context, I want to talk about how we can implement this into our ability to gain true success. I was practicing the techniques and skills from the works I mentioned earlier for about three years when I came to the conclusion I just mentioned to you. At this point, I started going back through what has been up to this point an affirmation/afformation list for each area of my life. We will talk about the rest of the steps we need to go through in a bit, but we have to dig deep here because we are laying a foundation for everything we are going to build upon. If we don't have a firm foundation, the building will not stand. So, if you look at it from the view of a building, the foundation is made up of a desperate, burning desire and definiteness of purpose that is intentional in focus and faith.

What I discovered is the answer to the question. If I'd set my mind/desire on the goal (Hill, 2000), affirmed and visualized it (Elrod, 2014), had the belief that I could accomplish it (Olson, 2013), maintained a clear focus on when I wanted to accomplish it (Jeary, 2009), and used "Why?" questions to bridge the gap between my subconscious and conscious (St. John, 2006), then my mind was working at its highest capacity. The God-given brain I had was using its RAS to transport thoughts and change beliefs from my subconscious to my conscious. St John's (2006) discovery of how the questions are used to open the brain and make it search for an answer is brilliant. What I realized is that once your brain is open to the question and searching for an answer, I was able to give it the answer. I used scriptures to answer the questions my brain was searching for. Let's take a look at the example we looked at before:

Hill's desire – I want to… lose 20 pounds.
Eldrod's affirmation – I will… lose 20 pounds.
Nightingale's thoughts – I think and decide… I will lose 20 pounds.

Olson's philosophy – I believe I can…. lose 20 pounds.
Jeary's clarity – I will…. lose 20 pounds by December 31, 2016.
St. John's use of questions – Why am I having such success losing weight and meeting my goal of losing 20-pounds by the end of the year?
Add scriptures – 1 Corinthians 6:19-20:
"Do you not know that your bodies are temples of the Holy Spirit, who is in you, whom you have received from God? You are not your own. For you have been bought with a price: therefore glorify God in your body."

Scriptures locked in the answer. My brain was open, searching and looking for the answer to the goal that I was intentionally setting my mind to go after. I had an intense desire to accomplish the goal, had a definiteness of purpose, affirmed with words what my goals were about that topic and clearly defined goals and dates set to accomplish them, believing that I had set realistic and attainable goals. I used questions to open my mind and start pushing the new information through my subconscious, and then I locked it in with scriptures that gave me the answer.

Without question, I can say that the difference in my mind and the physiological reaction in my body were immediate. Day after day, my intentionality, my focus, my clarity, my belief, my confidence and my unwavering faith grew in my ability to accomplish every goal I set for myself. I have quickly seen the benefits of this system with those I have talked with. They have raved about how this was the answer for them, giving them what it was going to take to get to the goals they were setting for themselves.

I have to a make a small caveat about the word "why." I want to make clear that when we are using the questions starting with "why" during the afformation process, we are not using it to question in a negative way but in an positive way for opening up possibilities. Also, with God we do not want to arrogantly, negatively come before Him and ask "Why?" When we do this, we are actually stepping into a position of authority and control and acting as if God is supposed to answer to us. We should have a humble heart and ask God to help us see or understand things. The key is the heart with which we are asking.

As I mentioned earlier, this is the foundation. If you want to have the true success we are discussing and create a plan for each area of your life, it will be most beneficial for you to not move forward until you have mastered these concepts! You need to have a clear mindedness about each area you intend to focus on. If you do not build on the solid foundation, the building will fall. If you build on the rock, even the wind and the waves will not be able to move you.

3. THOUGHTS

Whenever someone mentions the word *thought*, I imagine what runs through your mind is what you think about. There are many famous quotes on the subject of *thoughts*:

"Thoughts are Things." – Napoleon Hill

"You are what you think." – Buddha

"Whether you think you can or think you can't, you're right." – Henry Ford

While it is true that we have thoughts come through our minds, I want to talk about thoughts in regards to the heart. Have you ever heard someone say they are going to listen to their heart? Well, they may have been more correct than what they even realized.

Let's look at a few scriptures that help make it clearer.

Genesis 6:5-6 – "The LORD saw how great the wickedness of the human race had become on the earth, and that every inclination of the thoughts of the human heart was only evil all the time. The LORD regretted that he had made human beings on the earth, and his heart was deeply troubled." *Man's heart was evil. God's heart was grieved.*

1 Chronicles 28:9 – "And you, my son Solomon, acknowledge the God of your father, and serve him with wholehearted devotion and with a willing mind, for

the LORD searches every heart and understands every desire and every thought. If you seek him, he will be found by you; but if you forsake him, he will reject you forever." *This scripture lets us know that God searches our heart and understands the desires and thoughts in it.*

Hebrews 4:12 – "For the word of God is alive and active. Sharper than any double-edged sword, it penetrates even to dividing soul and spirit, joints and marrow; it judges the thoughts and attitudes of the heart." *It talks about us having thoughts and attitudes of the heart.*

Mark 7:20-22 – "He went on: 'What comes out of a person is what defiles them. For it is from within, out of a person's heart, that evil thoughts come—sexual immorality, theft, murder, adultery, greed, malice, deceit, lewdness, envy, slander, arrogance and folly.'" *Again, the scripture describes evil thoughts coming from a person's heart.*

Luke 6:45 – "The good man out of the good treasure of his heart brings forth what is good; and the evil man out of the evil treasure brings forth what is evil; for his mouth speaks from that which fills his heart" (NASB). *This scripture is telling us that the mouth speaks what comes from the heart.*

Somehow, before one thinks with his mind, he thinks with his heart and these deep, unspoken thoughts will determine the way he reasons with his brain. This helps us understand why things come out of our mouth before we actually think about them with our minds. The heart is driving the thought and some feeling or idea is attached to it.

There have been many books written on how important and powerful our thoughts are. As you examine what we have discussed, you see that our thoughts are paramount in determining our destiny. Have you ever taken the time to study how to overcome your thoughts, how to control or change them?

No matter what kind of goal you have set for yourself, you have to take the time to think about what your thoughts are for that specific topic. As we discussed, scriptures answer those questions as you open up your mind and search for an answer.

Along with the thoughts in our hearts, we know we have thoughts in our minds. We have to make a decision to handle the thoughts of our minds. We will discuss the mind and its thoughts in the next section. For now, we are talking about the heart and its motives and motivations.

One of the first things we need to tackle in regards to this is what I will call the trash, remnants, sin and struggles we have in our hearts. We cannot ignore the trash because it is going to rot us from the inside out. We must be willing to take out the trash and rid ourselves of anything needing to be thrown out. If you look at it from this perspective, then it seems clear why we need to change bad attitudes, negative thinking and ill feelings towards others, along with anything that keeps us from purifying ourselves. You have to determine you are willing to give up those things that are the trash in your life in order to experience joy beyond understanding, peace beyond measure and blessings beyond comprehension.

Another way we can look at our hearts is viewing it like a garden. We have to work the garden every day. We have to till it, plant seeds, water it, weed it and only then will we reap a harvest. One of the things that helped me was realizing that when our thoughts are negative, critical, self-focused, depressed and arrogant, we have to pull those weeds up or they will choke out the good seeds planted and we won't be able to have a harvest. When we think those thoughts, we are also participating in things of this world. We are trapped in this world and what it can produce. We also tend to look down and inward, our countenance changes and the energy in our body changes, which pulls us down.

When we change our thinking and focus on the positive (love, joy, peace, patience, kindness, goodness, faithfulness and self-control), we are thinking about things above, things that are blessings from God. We are focusing outward and we are lighter in our step, have a bigger smile on our face and a twinkle in our eyes. We are planting good seeds, not weeds. And, we will reap a harvest from those things.

You may know what it feels like to have something coming over you, wanting to drag you down into that pit. You may feel like it is overcoming you or overwhelming you with feelings. When I feel that happening, I stop what I am doing and start praying. I remind myself that I am going to focus on things above, that I am going to set my mind on Jesus and I am not going to be dragged away and wallow in self pity, guilt or shame. I want to focus on what is going to build me up in my mind to do good works. By praying out loud, if possible, scriptures, positive words, affirming words, we can kick RAS into gear and work to overcome what is happening to us at that moment. We are actually able to, in a sense, step outside ourselves and rise above the situation we are dealing with.

Philippians 4:8 says, "Finally, brothers, whatever is true, whatever is honorable, whatever is just, whatever is pure, whatever is lovely, whatever is commendable, if there is any excellence, if there is anything worthy of praise, think about these things" (ESV).

So when I start to struggle, I remind myself that I need to think about what is true, what is just, what is pure. Sometimes when there are very extreme circumstances going on this can be very difficult to do, which is why you have to pray. When you pray, crying out to God to save you from whatever is trying to get ahold of you, you will be able to work it out. If you read through Psalms, David spends a lot of time crying out to God. He cried out when his son was trying to kill him, when Saul was trying to kill him, when he had to flee from his castle, when he felt all alone. If you look closely, David spends his time crying out about how he feels but, towards the end of the psalms, he changes the focus. He starts reminding himself of who God is, talking to God and praising God for all he has done and, by the end of the psalm, he has worked it out. With the exception of Psalm 88, David's mind focuses on looking to and relying on God to take care of and protect him.

It doesn't matter if you are having issues at work with a co-worker, your boss or an employee. It doesn't matter if you are trying to become more successful and overcome things in your character to help you get to the next level. It doesn't matter if you are having problems with your spouse or kids. The principle is the same. If you give it to God, He will answer you. He will provide a way to deal with whatever it is you are going through.

1 Corinthians 10:13 – "No temptation has overtaken you except what is common to mankind. And God is faithful; he will not let you be tempted beyond what you can bear. But when you are tempted, he will also provide a way out so that you can endure it" (NIV).

Remember that thoughts are things and what you think is what you become. You have to decide what you want to become. You have to be willing to deal with your thoughts to have the life you dream of, the marriage you hope for and the relationships you long for. It is possible.

At this point, take time to write down any thoughts that need to change. Take time to figure out where you came up with that limiting belief. Think through what you need to replace that thought with, what the positive is in place of that thought. Decide that you are not going to allow other people to have control of your thoughts or to determine how you see yourself. I had to choose to stop believing the things said about me and start believing the things my

Father in heaven believed about me. I had to quit believing the lies and the limiting beliefs and stop giving a man the power to control my thoughts. I chose to change the way I thought and, as a result, have changed my life.

4. ATTITUDES

Attitude – a settled way of thinking or "feeling" about someone or something, typically one that is reflected in a person's behavior; a position of the body proper to or implying an action or mental state (*Google*, n.d.).

"You attitude, not your aptitude, will determine your altitude." – Zig Ziglar

Napoleon Hill (2000) says, "The world is ruled, and the destiny of civilization is established, by the human emotions. People are influenced in their actions, not by reason so much as by 'feelings.'" The creative faculty of the mind is set into action entirely by emotions, and not by cold reason.

Our attitudes are our feelings about things. The way we act or react about situations comes from the attitudes or feelings we have about that situation or people involved.

Hebrews 4:12 – "For the word of God is alive and active. Sharper than any double-edged sword, it penetrates even to dividing soul and spirit, joints and marrow; it judges the thoughts and attitudes of the heart."

If the Bible is going to judge the thoughts and attitudes of the heart, we need to take the time to examine what is going on inside us. Many times people are not successful simply because they don't "feel" like doing something. They allow their feelings to dictate their actions instead of the other way around.

When you think about how our feelings can get us into trouble, it makes a lot of sense when we read a passage like Jeremiah 17:9, which says, “The heart is deceitful above all things, and desperately sick; who can understand it?” (ESV).

We have to understand that our hearts, which are where our feelings and attitudes come from, are deceitful and ruled by emotion. We can’t assume that everything we feel is correct, which is why the scripture says it is deceitful above all things. That should give us the hint that our feelings can and many times are very deceitful and very wrong.

If we are going to change, we can’t allow our feelings to control us. We have to master our feelings and emotions, the thoughts and attitudes of our heart. God doesn’t tell us to see how we feel about it and then do what we feel. He tells us we need to obey.

That’s it. Obedience doesn’t have to do with feelings. It has to do with doing what is right, no matter how you feel.

There is an old saying, “Do what is right and your heart will follow.” It is supporting the decision to obey and do the right thing and eventually the emotions, feelings and attitudes of your heart will follow.

This will come in very handy when we get attitudes about people or with people. We can remind ourselves that our heart is deceitful and that we can't necessarily trust our feelings. We can check our feelings against the word of God and see if we are in line with obedience to Him. If we are not, then we need to wrestle with and master the feeling to bring it into line with what is right. This will probably be one of the hardest things you work on since feelings can be so overwhelming and consuming but, with scriptures to fight them and your actions of obedience to back them up, you will experience a victory.

When I was praying, God pulled it all together for me. As we learned, our hearts are where our desires and our feelings are. When you think about what happens when you wind up in a bad situation or start struggling with something, normally you start having those overwhelming feelings, you start feeling like you are being dragged into a pit, you start getting overwhelmed or anxious and worried. What is happening is your heart is going full force with the feelings and desires raging inside you.

As you are going to learn about in the next section, we are going to find out how to take control of our minds. Our hearts are the feeling and emotional side of us, and our minds are the logical, rational side of us. You have two opposing forces going at each other when you are in a tough situation. The key is to learn to use the mind you have been given to overcome and tame your heart. You have to gain the skill by using your intelligence, your brain, your knowledge and your understanding to overcome the raw emotions, desires, lusts and feelings of the heart. By doing what we discussed in the last section, laying out your desires, your affirmations, your clarity, your beliefs, your questions and your scriptures, you are able to determine how to deal with each difficult area your heart tends to drag you away on. You are able to literally accomplish "mind over matter" when it comes to these matters of the heart.

This is a huge awakening for me since I have times where I get bad news that I can be dragged away and consumed with my feelings, my situation, my circumstances and the day is swept away from me. By understanding that I have to stop and use my mind to overcome these emotions, I can control my mind and my mind can control my actions.

For example, let's say something happens at work and it kicks up something in me and I start to worry. Worry is a feeling in my heart, an emotion. When I feel it, I have to stop myself and say that it is just a feeling and it is not going to control me. I have scriptures ready to pray through I had prepared when I laid out my affirmations and the things in my character I wanted to overcome. If I have my affirmation list on my phone, I can open it up and pray through that section again. I have to refocus my mind and decide I am not going to give in to that feeling. I have to make a choice to focus on what I need to be focused on instead of worrying. It is a process you can go through for any feeling you struggle with: fear, anger, anxiety, smoking, etc. I have a girlfriend I taught this technique to and she has been able to overcome her temptation to smoke. It works because you are making a decision that you are not going to allow your feelings to control you, but you are going to be prepared in your mind to take control of your emotions and actions.

Another way of looking at it is that you can spend your time in the morning pouring your heart out to God in prayer, crying, being vulnerable and open. Then when you get up from your prayer time, you are going to close the door to your heart and let your brain work for the day to make the decisions you need to make to live the life you have chosen to live. Not meaning that you are going to be unloving or cold, but think about it in the way that you open your heart up when you are with God in private or studying the Bible. Other than that you have closed the door for your heart to run wild and run your day. Many people spend their entire day run by their emotions. It's like they left their brain at home. That is when you see people cutting each other off on the road, or road rage. You see people screaming at each other. If they had left the emotionally charged heart at home and made logical and rational decisions, they wouldn't be out of control and living in chaos.

There is an old saying about wearing your heart on your sleeve. This is not who we are destined to be. We are destined to be like Jesus. While He loved intensely and poured Himself out for people, He was not ruled by His emotions and had focused, intentional daily decisions that worked towards His goal.

This will be a huge factor when you start going up against the things you want to change. You have to train yourself and your mind to determine the outcome of your way of life.

III. WRAPPING YOUR HEAD AROUND IT

1. MINDSET

Mindset - a particular way of thinking; a person's attitude or set of opinions about something; a fixed state of mind (*Google*, n.d.).

"If you don't think you can do it, who will? You control the most important tool in success, your mind." - Jeffrey Gitomer

We talked in a previous section about how important it is to take your thoughts captive and how your thoughts determine who you become. Thus, it is extremely important for you to have the right mindset.

Mindset is an established set of attitudes held by someone. It may seem a little confusing but it all works together so seamlessly that it seems like it is just one thing, but there are multiple things that have to be evaluated to make sure you are going after it the more effective way.

As we learned, your attitudes are the feelings of your heart. We learned that we can be dragged away or enticed by the desires in our hearts and do things we really don't want to do. We then learned that our thoughts determine who we become.

We have to bring all of these things in line with each other and set our minds the way we want them to be set. To figure out what you really desire in your heart, we need to deal with our bad desires to make sure we aren't taken off the path we want to go on, then we need to wrestle through old patterns of thought and come up with a plan of what we are going to decide to think and how we are going to decide to think. It may seem a little overwhelming at first, but once you start breaking it all down and laying it out on paper, it will get easier. Sometimes the hardest thing is beginning.

For example, if I want to be more successful, I have to figure out what my desire for the success is. Do I want to have a lot of money or do I simply care about taking care of my family? Do I want to own a company and lead other people or do I want to have a nine to five job and not have to work weekends? Depending on what my desire is for that subject, I then have to figure out what exactly I'm going to go after. I have to deal with old feelings or thoughts of failure, being too old to start or too old to go back to school to learn something new. I have to deal with possible criticism from other people on changing the direction of my career. I have known many people who go back to school in their fifties to become the doctor or whomever they want to be. One of the oldest gentlemen I met was 80 years old and had just gotten his real estate license, making a business plan for how many houses he wanted to sell that year. As well, Hill (2000) discusses how most of the truly successful people he interviewed came into success well into their forties or fifties.

As the definition describes, it is a setting of the mind, an established set of attitudes, a determining what you are going to do, a making of choices you need to make to accomplish your goal. It isn't saying, "let's hope for the best" or "let's see if it happens" attitude. It is a specific and decisive conviction of a pre-determined course of action that you follow to accomplish your goals. To set something, you direct it with fixed attention. It takes energy and attention. It takes your focus. It takes the intentional decision of what you intend to do or accomplish.

One of the scriptures that helps me the most is Colossians 3:2 that says, "Set your minds on things above, not on earthly things."

If our thoughts are things and what we think about determines who we become, then it all comes down to what we set our mind on, what we focus on. This is especially important, since we learned in the last chapter, that we are able to use our minds to overcome our emotions and change the course of destiny in our lives.

FOCUS

Focus – producing clear vision, pay particular attention to, center of attention, focal point (*Dictionary.com*, n.d.).

Robert T. Kiyosaki (2013), in "Why We Want You To Be Rich," says:
Follow
One
Course
Until
Successful (Kiyosaki & Trump, 2013)

Your focus will determine your reality. Socrates says, "The secret of change is to focus all of your energy, not on fighting the old, but on building the new."

"Success at anything will always come down to this: focus and effort. And we control both." – Dwayne "The Rock" Johnson

"Your life is controlled by what you focus on." – Anthony Robbins

Proverbs 4:25-27 says, "Let your eyes look straight ahead; fix your gaze directly before you. Give careful thought to the paths for your feet and be steadfast in all your ways. Do not turn to the right or the left; keep your foot from evil."

Have you ever looked through a pair of binoculars or a telescope on a rifle aimed at a bull's-eye. It is amazing how far you can see, how clear your vision becomes. Everything is brought into plain view. You get to watch exactly what you are aiming at, what you are trying to get a glimpse of. You have pinpointed with precise precision your target.

What you don't think about is all of the other things you can't see or don't see. Naturally, our eyes have peripheral vision, which gives us the ability to take in almost 180 degrees of sight line. We naturally assimilate information about everything that is in our line of sight, without even giving it much thought. We can see if our eye catches something that is being thrown at us or could cause us danger. It is a natural reaction.

That is the incredible power of focus. It gives us clear vision, takes away all of the peripheral distractions. Then looking down that barrel, it brings our target into perfect sight for us to aim, fire and hit the bull's-eye.

In every area of our lives, we have to have laser focus on what we are aiming at. As Zig Ziglar states, "If you aim at nothing, you will hit it every time."

Paul tells us in 1 Corinthians 9:26, "Therefore I do not run like someone running aimlessly; I do not fight like a boxer beating the air" (NIV).

Following God means that instead of concentrating on how you feel, you focus on what you know to be true from the Word of God. You focus on what you are going to be and do for God. You focus on what you will master and change in your life. This laser focus will allow us to not be the people described in Ephesians 4:14, "Then we will no longer be infants, tossed back and forth by the waves, and blown here and there by every wind of teaching and by the cunning and craftiness of people in their deceitful scheming."

Your focus will bring clarity to your goals, vision and mission and will determine the steps you take towards changing your life. This works in every area of your life, at whatever you decide to master.

Ralph Waldo Emerson says, "Do the thing and you shall have the power." This is where you can be if you are willing to focus on doing the actions each day to get you there. A book that helps bring focus is Jeff Olson's (2013) "The Slight Edge: Secret to a Successful Life." He talks about bringing everything into focus, about creating your philosophy and ultimately the life you want (Olson, 2013).

A very encouraging quote for me is, "Life is like a camera, just focus on what's important, capture the good times, develop from the negatives and if things don't work out, just take another shot."

Focus <u>Is</u> what matters, so focus <u>On</u> what matters.

2. LOOSEN THE NOTS

In order to have your focus clear and intentional, you may need to loosen the NOTS.

What are your nots? Your "can't, won't, don't want to" attitude or your "can't make me" mentality? We all have had those defeating conversations or down on yourself pity-parties. Maybe it is due to the circumstance or situation you are in, or maybe it is just in your mind. Maybe you are naturally negative, with an Eyeore-type personality.

To become a success in your destined field or any endeavor in your life, the first battle is going to be overcoming any negative thoughts in your mind. This is probably the hardest thing for most people to overcome and probably the reason why more people aren't successful. My coach calls it the "drunk monkey" in your head, telling you all the reasons why you can't do the thing that you desire to do or accomplish.

Normally, if you dig deep, you will realize that those NOTS are being motivated or coming from fear. Fear of change, fear of success or fear of failure. We will get to fear in a little bit, but let's talk about the NOTS.

This is where you have to take the time to figure out what your nots are and start to replace them. One of the most powerful ways to overcome your thinking is to start to replace it with positive thoughts. I am talking about scientific breakthroughs in the study of the brain and how it translates into your life. There are numerous books you can read on this topic but, as we learned in the last chapter, Hill (2000) says, "Thoughts are things" (p. 27).

Hill (2000) says to work on the following:
Not I will try but I WILL DO, I WILL BE, and I WILL SEE, Not I will quit but I WILL NEVER QUIT.

Not only did Hill (2000) talk about setting out to overcome the negative or nots in your brain but to write out the choice or affirmation to the not. Then the key is to repeat those affirmations every day, twice a day, until your mind eventually convinces itself of that truth.

There was a study done about the number of times we are told no by our parents before we grew up that was astounding. So, it makes sense why we have such a hard time overcoming the not's since we have "no" drilled into our heads from the time we are children.

Hill (2000) says, "Every man is what he is because of the dominating thoughts he permits to occupy his mind…Thoughts which a man deliberately places in his own mind, and encourages with sympathy, mix with emotions, is the motivating forces which direct and control his every movement, act and deed" (p. 108).

We have the ability to make choices in our lives, to say "yes" to the right things and "no" to the wrong things. We can set ourselves up for success in each area of our lives and be overcomers. The scripture I hang on to when I start feeling the pull of the not's is Titus 2:12 says, "It teaches us to say 'no' to ungodliness and worldly passions, and to live self-controlled, upright and godly lives in this present age." I tell myself "No, I am not going to think that or do that. I am not going to give up. I choose to say 'No.'"

I know you have heard the idiom *mind over matter*. Well, they were right, it is mind over matter. You have to train your mind to overcome the matter, which is what is rolling around in your head and heart. Once you work and sift out what is going on in your head and heart to bring them in line, you will be surprised how easy it is to get your body going.

You will have to figure out what your not's are. Mine, when they rear their ugly head, come through as doubts, fears and insecurities – I can't do this; I will never be able to get this done; I won't be good at that.

Not is one of the most destructive words in our English language. But, it can become a very powerful word if you turn it around and use it as a motivator. Instead, start saying, "I will not do that, I will not give in, I will not allow you to treat me that way, I will not accept that."

Sometimes, based on your past experiences, this can be an area you have to wrestle through. This can free you from the chains you feel hold you back from becoming everything you can be. Take your time and be patient with yourself. This is a process, not an event. Enjoy the process of growing and transforming as you go.

3. CUT THE STRINGS

Once you have loosened the not's, you will have to decide to cut the strings.

2 Corinthians 10:5 says, "We demolish arguments and every pretension that sets itself up against the knowledge of God, and we take captive every thought to make it obedient to Christ."

To take captive, you make the choice, you control it, and you decide what you are going to think. You make your thoughts obedient to Christ. You have to figure out what that is, how to obey, how to follow, how to imitate Him, how to become like Him. You have to decide based on how desperate you are and how much you desire to change, that you are going to tackle your thoughts.

Romans 12:2 instructs us, saying, "Do not conform to the pattern of this world, but be transformed by the renewing of your mind. Then you will be able to test and approve what God's will is—his good, pleasing and perfect will."

You have to be transformed. You need a 'mind change' by Jesus, God and the Holy Spirit. You have to allow yourself to experience a paradigm shift. You will be able to renew your mind, make it new, completely different. Then the amazing part is that God starts working to open your eyes, to help you test and approve what His will is. Once He sees that you are fighting to change and shift your mind over to

His way and follow Him, He will step up and show you the way.

Imagine a parent teaching a baby to walk. The baby is distracted, looking all over, not really into it. The parent is patiently waiting, calling out to him, trying to get his attention. Then the baby locks in and starts attempting to walk, shifting his focus and mind onto his parent and making an effort to go towards them. Once that happens the parents are all in, cheering them on, clapping shouts of joy at every step the baby makes.

It is no different with God. He wants to see our effort; He wants us to reach out to Him. He wants to know we are focused and determined to come His way, to come to Him. Once He sees the effort, He is on His feet; legions of angels are cheering you on, shouting for joy at every step and every effort you make.

Hebrews 12:1-2 says, "Therefore, since we have so great a cloud of witnesses surrounding us, let us also lay aside every encumbrance and the sin which so easily entangles us, and let us run with endurance the race that is set before us, fixing our eyes on Jesus, the author and perfecter of faith, who for the joy set before Him endured the cross, despising the shame, and has sat down at the right hand of the throne of God" (NASB).

We have to cut the strings on the things that easily entangle us, which is how we have to handle those nots. I think about it like a puppet. Satan is using us as his puppets; to dance the way he wants us to and lead us to where he wants us to go. You have to cut the strings, stop being controlled by him or other factors. In your mind, imagine taking an axe to the things that make you struggle in order to cut them off. You aren't going to allow them to control you any more.

I found this picture, which is the perfect example of what is happening.

2 Peter 2:20 says, "If they have escaped the corruption of the world by knowing our Lord and Savior Jesus Christ and are again entangled in it and are overcome, they are worse off at the end than they were at the beginning" (NIV). If you keep going back and forth like a yo-yo, making attempts to change and do what is right and then giving in and going back to what you did before, you will actually wind up worse off than before you began.
The thought of the devil having strings on me and pulling them to make me do what he wants infuriates me. It fires me up and makes me want to cut those strings. I don't want him to have control over me. I don't want to be the devil's puppet but that is exactly what happens when we aren't intentionally making every choice, every day about who we are going to be and what we are going to do.

I can choose to cut those strings and choose to obey God. I like the song Pinocchio sings:

"I've got no strings to hold me down
To make me fret, or make me frown

I had strings but now I'm free
There are no strings on me
I'm as happy as can be
Nothing ever worries me
There ain't no strings on me." (Luske et al., 1940)

As we discussed when we talked about being desperate, the people who really make changes are people who are desperate, have that burning desire to change and then put all of their focus into changing whatever it is. If you are not there, you need to spend some time figuring out why you aren't.

If you really want a different life, there are going to be things you have to cutout of your life and cut off in order to make the changes necessary for true success. What is it that is stopping you from getting to that point to be able to make the changes needed to get to where you want to be?
We have to be clear that there are only two choices in this life. We can either serve God or serve the devil. I'm not sure if you have ever thought about or realized that. We all act like we are in control of our lives but in reality we are not. We are either bowing before the throne of the devil every time we live in our sin or we choose to stop serving him and turn around and bow before the throne of God. There is no middle ground, there is no "my way." Just as there is light or dark, good or evil, right or wrong, heaven or hell, there is no gray area, no half way. While that is absolute truth, there are the feelings and times of struggle working to get from one to the other. There are moments where you haven't gotten it, figured it out, or been able to

master something, but the effort of obedience is there, going in the right direction.

As I was praying today, God showed me a very clear picture of what happens to us. I was praying and talking to God about the things He put on my heart that I needed to repent of and change from the day before. He put a picture and scene in my mind. The scene was of me in a pigpen, rolling around in the mud and then immediately He put a scene of me lying in a garbage dump, rolling around in the trash. This is what we do when we are in sin. We are rolling around in the trash pile, hugging the trash, smelling the trash, enjoying it, reveling in it, eating it and filling our stomachs with it as if it was the finest restaurant we have ever been to.

As we reveled and consumed our trash, we heard a noise. We heard what sounds like a party, music going, voices singing, clapping, laughing and people having a great time. We got up out of our trash pile and realized we couldn't go to the party all stinky, dirty and disgusting. We ran into the bathroom and took off all of the dirty clothes, shower and scrub ourselves from top to bottom until we are squeaky-clean. Luckily, there was a clean set of clothes there for us to put on. We weren't sure whose party it was, but we wanted to be a part of it. We walked through the gates and saw all of the most glorious looking people, smiles on their faces, laughing, joking around, and having an amazing time. We have never seen people so happy. At first we felt really awkward, out of place. It actually made us uncomfortable because we just came from the trash pile, rolling around and reveling in our garbage. We looked and saw table after table of the most amazing food we had ever seen, we couldn't even believe how delicious it looked. We walked over to one of them and got a little plate. Oh my goodness, how delightful. We had never tasted anything so amazing, the meat melted in our mouths, the fruits were so sweet and juicy they made our mouths water. We felt like we were in heaven.

All of a sudden someone put a hand on our shoulder. When we turned around, we were greeted with the biggest smile, the warmest eyes and could feel a love pouring out from Him that felt like He just wrapped a blanket around us. He said He wondered where we had been and was so happy we finally made it. I realized He was raising His arm up and when I finally caught a glimpse of what He was doing, my mouth fell wide open and I started to pull away. He gently grabbed my arm and said, "This is for you." He put a crown on my head, put His arm around me and turned out towards the crowd of people at the party. Before I could do anything, He started speaking to the crowds and explained to them that His daughter had finally come home and He was so pleased that He could introduce me to everyone. As everyone applauded and cheered it sounded like the applause of heaven, like when you are in an NFL football game or a packed concert and the crowd goes wild for the team or performer. It literally sounded like 10,000 angels were cheering, and they were doing it for me. When things settled down a little bit, He turned and looked at me and said, "Welcome home, my princess, I love you."

Do you realize that is what *you* have in store for you? You are wallowing around in your trash pile, eating garbage and pig slop. There is a party waiting for you with you as the guest of honor and they are waiting for you to be crowned by the King. Your part is to make the effort, get out of the trash, and go wash yourself off, and get dressed and ready for the party. The rest is already taken care of and prepared for you. You can stop bowing before a fake king who destroys you. Instead, you can bow before the true King and be crowned with all of His glory and splendor. I, for one, have chosen the later.

4. AUTOSUGGESTION AND VISUALIZATION

A few of the tools useful in assisting you in your journey to change are autosuggestion and visualization.

Autosuggestion is the hypnotic or subconscious adoption of an idea that one has originated oneself (e.g. through repetition of verbal statements to oneself in order to change behavior) (*Oxford Dictionaries*, n.d.).

Visualization is the formation of mental visual images; the act or process of interpreting in visual terms or of putting into visible form (*Merriam-Webster* online dictionary, n.d.).

There are many books, articles, blogs and studies that have expanded on the power of these tools to assist you in your ability to change. Predominately, it comes through the research about repetition of a thought or action in order to convince your mind, or bring your mind into a change through constant repetition. These techniques are used and taught by many professional business trainers.

Hill (2000) explains that this is the medium for influencing the subconscious mind. He describes that it is a self-suggestion (Hill, 2000). It is the link between the conscious and subconscious mind. He emphasizes that no thought can enter the subconscious mind without the aid of autosuggestion (Hill, 2000). He explains that the conscious mind is a guard that stops thoughts from entering, unless we allow them (Hill, 2000). He describes the power that man has to have complete control over what goes into the subconscious mind (Hill, 2000).

He describes your subconscious as a garden through which autosuggestion plant the seeds of success and greatness or seeds of destruction (Hill, 2000). He concluded that by repeating the affirmations and written statements of your desires out loud that eventually your conscious mind convinces your subconscious it is true (Hill, 2000). Hill notes that a mere reading of the statements is of no value, unless mixed with emotions, which he calls faith (Hill, 2000). He says you have to have statements that have been well emotionalized with belief (Hill, 2000).

Hill describes faith as a state of mind which may be induced or created by affirmation or repeated instructions to the subconscious mind through the principle of autosuggestion (Hill, 2000). As we described earlier in the section on desires, as Christians, we have a different view of what faith means. I do believe many of the things Hill talks about are absolutely factual and helpful in obtaining the worldly goals you desire. If you just want to get rich, which is what he teaches you the concepts for, then that is enough for you to have a successful, wildly profitable life on this earth. But if you want true success, which will include not only an amazingly blessed life on this earth but an amazingly close relationship with God here and in the future, then you have to take it one step farther.

Faith is what Hebrews 11:1 describes as, "Now faith is confidence in what we hope for and assurance about what we do not see."

It is a confidence, a security, taking the first step, taking a leap with the trust that you will be okay. Faith makes things possible; it is trusting in His will. Feed your faith and your fears will starve to death. Faith breeds fearlessness.

I like a quote by Philip Yancey that says, "I have learned that faith means trusting in advance what will only make sense in reverse."

Faith is what is needed most and what is sometimes understood least. What helped me grow in my faith was understanding where it comes from and how to get it, which we described earlier. It is worth repeating the two scriptures, Romans 10:17 and Hebrews 12:2. Romans 10:17 says, "Consequently, faith comes from hearing the message, and the message is heard through the Word about Christ." Hebrews 12:2 says, "Fixing our eyes on Jesus, the author and perfecter of faith, who for the joy set before Him endured the cross, despising the shame, and has sat down at the right hand of the throne of God" (NASB).

There is nothing that you can't overcome when you build up your faith in Him. In Matthew 21:21, "Jesus replied, 'Truly I tell you, if you have faith and do not doubt, not only can you do what was done to the fig tree, but also you can say to this mountain, 'Go, throw yourself into the sea,' and it will be done'" (NIV).

We can use autosuggestion to plant seeds or suggestions in

our subconscious to change our beliefs. We must recognize the concept of using the scriptures to plant the seeds of faith, seeds of fearlessness, seeds of confidence, security and trust. There isn't a seed that I can't plant in my mind to help me overcome whatever obstacle I am facing. Over time, through focus, prayer and repetition, my mind eventually changes.

Visualization is the picturing of success or transformation in your mind. See yourself accomplishing the actions. See how you will look, how you will feel, how wonderful the end result will be. You can take time to do this in a few minutes after you read each affirmation. You can stop to see the picture in your head and feel the feelings of what it is going to be like when you accomplish whichever goal you are focused on.

You will be able to use the techniques taught by Hill (2000), writing down your statements, goals, visions, desires and then reading them out loud, to allow your conscious to eventually grind them into your subconscious. You should add the scriptures, the Word of God for each of those goals, since that is where true faith will come from. This puts into play the power of what Hill (2000) describes having the emotions mixed with the thoughts to bring about success in every area of your life. As Christians and followers of Jesus, we can have true success and not just settle for success in this world.

You can also create a vision board where you cut out pictures for each area of your life. Each picture should be where you want to be and what you want to accomplish, so it shows the end result of what you are working towards. Then you arrange and paste the pictures onto a poster board and hang it up where you can see it and have the visual representation for what you are working on.

Both of these techniques are incredibly powerful and effective. They will bring the visual aspect in, which will fuel the flame of your desire. There are different learning styles, one of which is a visual learning process. For people with this learning style, it will be especially important for you to use these techniques in the process in order to bring yourself to your desired results.

5. IMAGINATION & SPECIALIZED KNOWLEDGE

Hill (2000) describes the need for both of these as the next step. Obviously, knowledge would be studying or gaining the information needed if you are setting specific goals in a field of study. This will take time and effort to work towards that goal.

"I fear not the man who has practiced 10,000 kicks once, but I fear the man who has practiced one kick 10,000 times." – Bruce Lee

In the book "Outliers: The Story of Success," author Malcolm Gladwell (2008) says that it takes roughly 10,000 hours of practice to achieve mastery in a field. Gladwell (2008) studied the lives of extremely successful people to find out how they achieved success. A surprising point emerged. They realized that there were no natural superstars in the groups studied. It all came down to hours in (Gladwell, 2008). The people that had become very successful had practiced two or three times more than the other people, which is what made them so much better. Gladwell (2008) gave an example of Bill Gates and Paul Allen, how they started practicing programming many years before they launched Microsoft and had completed at least 10,000 hours of programming. The Beatles practiced eight hours a day, seven days a week and completed 1,200 concerts before they burst onto the international music scene (Gladwell, 2008). He describes how the elite don't work harder than other people; they have just fallen in love with practicing their desired work (Gladwell, 2008).

With this thought in mind, when we set out our goals for each area of our lives and decide we are going to conquer areas of our lives, we have to remember we have to have the "time in" in order to achieve a high level of success in that area. This should help some of you if you are very impatient with yourself and you want everything to happen quickly. If you want something, determine the amount of time per day and per week you have to invest in it to achieve the desired level that you are looking for. This understanding should also encourage you in making decisions in how you manage your time. When you are focused on putting in the time and your desires become effortless and successful, you will use your time more wisely. You will realize your time has value. Every minute and every hour is worth something. It isn't something to be wasted or thrown away. It isn't something that I allow someone else to take or steal from me. I use my time as an investment in the pursuits and goals I have set for myself and allot my time efficiently in order to invest in what I am working towards. I will give you a copy of *My Perfect Day*, to give you an example of how to work towards scheduling your time in an intentional and focused way to work towards the goals you have set for yourself in each area of your life.

Imagination is needed for any goal you set. The imagination is important since this is where your ideas and dreams flourish. The greatest inventions of our time come from ideas. Spend time dreaming about what you want to accomplish in your life. Spend time thinking about the gifts

God has given you; the natural talents you have. Think how you can use them for Him, how you can do greater things than you had previously imagined because of what you are learning here. This is also called the faculty of imagining, which is the ability to form new images and sensations in the mind that are not perceived through senses such as sight or sound.

1 Corinthians 2:9 – "However, as it is written: What no eye has seen, what no ear has heard, and what no human mind has conceived – the things God has prepared for those who love him."

"If you can imagine it, you can achieve it. If you can dream it, you can become it." – William Arthur Ward

"I imagine that yes is the only living thing." – E. E. Cummings

Hill (2000) calls this the workshop of the mind. It is where all plans of man are created. Hill (2000) suggests that man's only limitation, within reason, lies in the development and use of his imagination. He focuses on the creative imagination, where dreams, hunches and inspirations come alive (Hill, 2000).

Through our imaginations, our subconscious can tune in and connect with other people's subconscious minds and create masterpieces. The key is to make use of these principles and put them into action. The key here is bringing those desires that we talked about, mixed with your emotions and faith, to work together to let your imagination run wild about what you can accomplish in each area of your life. The power of these things working together brings a force of nature that allows you to do what has never been done before!

Look at what great feats have been accomplished by men and women who had an idea about something being different, something being better. Look at what Jesus accomplished in His life and what continues to overflow to us. He started with a dream, a desire to see men freed from their bondage to sin, living a passionate, purposeful, powerful life for God, to offer true success.

God has used dreams and visions throughout the centuries to put ideas into men's hearts. All throughout the scriptures you read about the dreams and ideas that were given to men. Some of the greatest things that came about in the Bible were given through dreams but became reality. For me, this book was an idea He placed on my heart. Actually, He has put many ideas on my heart and in the last sixty days I have written two books, with an idea for a third one.

Psalm 126:1 "When the LORD restored the fortunes of Zion, we were like those who dreamed."

Hill (2000) describes the beginnings of Coca-Cola, J.C. Penney, Henry Ford, Einstein, Carnegie and the like. He details their lives, struggles, focus and ideas, which ultimately brought each of them great success and wealth in this life (Hill, 2000).

Ideas can be transmuted into cash; they can be poured out as blessings and packaged up as presents. The key is to take your dreams, ideas and imagination and put feet to them, put something into action. Do something about what God has put on your heart or given you talent to do. Don't let your dreams and ideas die; they may be the answer to someone else's prayers.

Hill (2000) says, "God seems to throw Himself on the side of the man who knows exactly what he wants, if he is determined to get JUST THAT!" (p. 207). What are you determined to get?

6. TRANSFORMED

"Things do not change. We change." – Henry David Thoreau

Romans 12:2 – "Do not conform to the pattern of this world, but be transformed by the renewing of your mind. Then you will be able to test and approve what God's will is – his good, pleasing and perfect will."

Let's talk about the Transformers. I'm not sure if you have ever watched that movie or have kids that were into them, but I have two boys who were raving fans. They released not only the movies, but there was a cartoon series, costumes and many toys available to purchase. Yes, my boys wanted all of it. They would dress up in the costumes and run around the house after each other. They would take all of the cars and trucks and go back and forth transforming them into the Autobots and Decepticons (appropriately named), battling each other for world domination.

If you think about it, that is how it is going to be. We are either going to be on the side of the Autobots, which are the good guys, or we are going to be on the side of the Decepticons, which are the bad guys. In the movies, you sometimes see some of the bad guys turn good or the good guys turn bad. But it is really clear that there are only two sides and you have to figure out which side you are fighting for.

Like the Transformers, we are going to be transformed into something. We will be useful and serve a purpose. If we are on the side of the Decepticons and really want to be on the side of the Autobots, get ready for battle. The full force of the dark side is going to come after you, tell you why you can't change, tell you why you don't want to go to the other side, tell you why you don't deserve it, that you will never make it or you aren't good enough to be on the good side. But, if you are willing to go to battle and fight through whatever it is that you need to fight through, you can get to the good side and start fighting for what is right, what is true, what is noble and what is pure.

If you were already on the side of the Autobots but you have a bad attitude, are ungrateful, critical, selfish, want things your way, think you know better, think everyone is stupid, think they are boring and it would be more fun to go to the other side, then you probably aren't far away from taking a trip down that road. You will be there before you know it, consumed by the darkness, filled with anger, rage and fury, eager to fight against everything that is good, true and right. You will have fun making fun of and humiliating the Autobots, attempting to do everything you can to destroy them because the sight of them – those goodie toe shoes who make you sick to your stomach.

God's hope is that you will be transformed into the likeness of His Son, becoming the radiance of Christ. His plan is to, like Ezekiel 36:26 says, "Moreover, I will give you a new heart and put a new spirit within you; and I will remove the heart of stone from your flesh and give you a heart of flesh"

(NASB). My prayer, as I struggle, has always been to allow Him to transform me. Psalm 51:10 says, "Create in me a clean heart, O God, and renew a steadfast spirit within me."

When you make the choice to come into the light and pick the right side, you take on all 2 Corinthians 5:17 says, "Therefore if anyone is in Christ, he is a new creature; the old things passed away; behold, new things have come."

Ephesians 4:22-24 – "That, in reference to your former manner of life, you lay aside the old self, which is being corrupted in accordance with the lusts of deceit, and that you be renewed in the spirit of your mind, and put on the new self, which in the likeness of God has been created in righteousness and holiness of the truth."

Colossians 1:21-23 – "And although you were formerly alienated and hostile in mind, engaged in evil deeds, yet He has now reconciled you in His fleshly body through death, in order to present you before Him holy and blameless and beyond reproach - if you continue in your faith, established and firm, and do not move from the hope held out in the gospel..."

You are a miracle! Your body is made up of approximately 60,000 miles of blood vessels ("Blood Vessels," 2016). You produce 200 billion new red blood cells every single day ("Blood Cell Formation," 2016). Your nose can remember 50,000 different scents ("Nose, Sinuses and Smell," 2016). You do not want to waste it by being focused on the wrong things.

"There are only two ways to live your life. One is as though nothing is a miracle. The other is as though everything is a miracle." – Albert Einstein

FEET TO FAITH THROUGH PLANNING

A part of being transformed is doing the thing you need to do to get you to that place. You have to figure out what your commitment to that topic/desire is going to be. This is where you are going to think through what it is going to take to get to your goal. Think about what effort, changes, calls, meetings, sacrifices, help from others or anything else it is going to take to get to your goal. Don't worry about not having everything you need right now. Don't worry about not being sure if you are missing something. It is amazing how ideas and opportunities start coming to us when we put into motion the actions necessary to achieve a particular goal.

This is the point where many people stop and don't pursue their goals. They feel it is too hard, too much work, too much time or too much effort. Well, if you think about it from the perspective that time does not stop, you are going to get older each day. But each day comes, whether we want it to or not. Time will pass and you will either be the same way you are right now or a little better and a little further ahead than where you are now. At least with the later situation you will be happy that you are at least making progress towards a worthy goal.

For example, if I want to lose 10 pounds by the end of the

year, I would think through the things that will help me reach my goal. Obviously, the first thing is what I eat, since 80% of weight loss is based on what goes into your body. I would have to think through a plan of what I want to eat that will help me reach my goal. If I have a meal plan a week in advance and know what I am going to fix for every meal, or even have it made prior to the start of the week, I will have much better success with sticking to my plan of how I want to eat. Then I would look at exercise and what I could do to work towards introducing exercise into my life. For people in very bad health, they may be limited to sitting in a chair and doing exercises or walking 20-30 minutes a day.

Lastly, I look up scriptures to support what it is I'm trying to accomplish. This is where the power comes in. I look for scriptures that support being a healthy weight, having a great marriage, growing in my relationship with God, being a great employee and being successful at everything I do.

Once all of this is written out in a clear and concise manner, you want to read through it every morning and every night. Laminate it, post it on your mirror or in your car and put a copy next to your bed.

You not only want to read it like you are reading a sentence off of a page but you want to imagine it, feel it, breath it in and believe that you are going to accomplish it. Believe and make a commitment that you are going to make small steps every day towards your goal. It may be saying no to the ice cream, putting that $30 in your retirement fund or not going to the party when you know there will be drinking. In whatever goals you have set for yourself, you are going to make focused, concerted choices each day to do something to get yourself to that goal.

IV. PUTTING IT ALL TOGETHER

"What you do speaks so loud I can't hear what you say!" – Ralph Waldo Emerson

Actions speak louder than words – you know how I feel about words. So if actions speak louder than words then how much more careful do we need to be about our actions?

ACTION

Once you have taken the time to figure out what it is you want to accomplish and how you are going to get there, then it comes down to putting it into practice. Surprisingly this is pretty easy if you have taken the time to really think through what you want, have the burning desire to accomplish it, make a specific plan of what needs to happen to get there and then you are just doing what you already made a decision and a commitment to do. I am not saying it is going to be easy, but the hard work and the struggle starts with figuring out what you want to do and become.

Once you have that burning desire, that definiteness of purpose and focus, you will be surprised how much easier it is to accomplish it. As you hone your skills and start accomplishing smaller things, you will also be amazed at how other opportunities open up to you. Success breeds success. It is a natural law of nature.

"Success requires no apologies. Failure permits to alibis."

– Napoleon Hill

You will also find that your attitude and mindset are changing as you start practicing this skill. You are going to be feeling happier and more confident. These are the positive benefits of being focused and having a definiteness of purpose.

No one exemplifies a definiteness of purpose more than Jesus. He was in heaven with God from the beginning (Gen. 1:26), He chose to come to the earth so that He could offer forgiveness of sins and the opportunity to spend eternity with God, He chose to be crucified for the forgiveness of our sins and was raised to life and sits at the right hand of God (Mark 16:19), crowned Lord of all (Phil. 2:11).

When you are working towards putting all of these things into action to accomplish your goals, you have to also be prepared for the obstacles or situations that may come up that will try to derail your success. We have seen the way we can use our desire to take us to the heights of success in each area of your life. Let's talk about how our desires can cause havoc and keep us enslaved to failure and misery.

James 1:14-15 – "But each person is tempted when they are dragged away by their own evil desires and enticed. Then, after desire has conceived, it gives birth to sin; and sin, when it is full-grown, gives birth to death" (NIV).

Genesis 4:7 – "If you do what is right, will you not be accepted? But if you do not do what is right, sin is crouching at your door; it desires to have you, but you must rule over it."

Galatians 5:16 – "So I say, walk by the Spirit, and you will not gratify the desires of the flesh."

James 4:2 – "You desire but you do not have, so you kill. You covet but you cannot get what you want, so you quarrel and fight. You do not have because you do not ask God."

The scripture in James 1 was my turning point. It was as if someone threw a bucket of cold water on me. At points throughout my life, I have made some very bad decisions and have had some circumstances that were the result of consequences from those decisions. I could not figure out how in the world I even got there. I obviously knew that I made that choice, but I couldn't figure out why. What in the world compelled me to do what I did? It was out of character for me and at a time in my life that it was not even on my radar as being something that mattered to me. Here I was, clueless as to what happened and trying to unravel it to figure out how to fix it; but more about that later.

Those I know who are alcoholics, they tell me they can't help it, that they don't want to do it, that they really want to quit. This is a perfect example of how there is some desire in them that drags them away and before they know it they are doing what they really don't want to do.

The scripture in Genesis 4 gives us the answer. It tells us that sin is at our door, it desires to have you, but you must rule over it, you must master it.

Most people don't take the time to think about what they really desire and don't understand the power of desire in their life – power to either give them their dreams or power to destroy those dreams.

It will be up to you to wrestle through all of your desires, to recognize what is good and profitable and will bring positive things into your life. You will also need to recognize the bad desires, how they will destroy your life if you let them and what you need to do to master them. You have to have a plan for both. If you don't have a plan, guess which one is going to win? If you don't take control of your life, your life will definitely take control of you.

Have you ever watched the television show "The Walking Dead"? Even though I haven't watched it, I have seen the commercials and I know it is a very popular show. This is what people are like. They are walking around every day, going to work, picking their kids up from soccer, attending PTA meetings, but they are really the walking dead. There is really no life in them, no purpose, no passion, no focus. By taking the time to pursue your dreams, discover your desires, explore and use your talents, you will come alive. You will be like the few in the show who aren't zombies but are working to stay away from the dead as well as find other people who are alive, who are human. That is exactly what happens when you start living. The floodgates are open for you, you meet other people striving to live the best life they can, you find people who are soaring in their lives. The kindred spirit of the other person who takes hold of their life and desires in order to master them will inspire you.

There is the story of Jesus raising Lazarus from the dead in John 11. Mark Batterson (2014), in his series "Grave Robber: How Jesus Can Make Your Impossible Possible," describes that we are no different from Lazarus, we are buried by our sin, our soul is wrapped in graves clothes. Jesus is calling us out, like He did Lazarus. He wants to raise us from the dead. He wants to give us a new life and body (Batterson, 2014).

It reminds me of the WWF or UFC. You are in the ring every day with the devil and he keeps taking you down. You keep tapping out, losing the fight. You can't seem to win. You cannot get up. No matter what you do, he is having victory over areas of your life. The problem is, you are fighting alone. Instead of tapping out, tap on Jesus' shoulder, grab ahold of the hem of Jesus' robe like the woman who was bleeding. You are already down, already being taken out. The bully is beating you up every day. It is time to get the big boy involved who can stand up for you, who can fight the battle for you. There is no reason you should ever lose a battle again if you are relying on the Defender, the Counselor and the Master to fight for you.

There is one particular killer that I want to point out that will be lurking in the dark once you take control of your life, your desires and start living your dreams. It is one of the main things that can get in your way and it can actually take away all of the work you have accomplished on your journey. It is contentment. Contentment kills desire. It lulls you to sleep without you even realizing it. It rocks you in the cradle and gently sways you, letting you know you have made it, that you can relax and enjoy your accomplishments. It is the silent killer that has made rich men poor. It is an enemy that you must always watch out for because it will extinguish the fire that is burning within you and it aims to steal your joy. There is nothing wrong with taking time to enjoy your life, bask in your success and celebrate your victories. You have to keep your passion, your fire and your burning desire to master yourself and your life and be constantly improving in each area of your life to gain the fullness and richness you desire.

I had a friend I was talking with who expressed wanting to be comfortable with where they went to church. That conversation kept rolling around in my head and as I continued praying about it, something hit me. God is absolutely the God of all comfort, who comforts us in our needs and all of our trials and struggles, as He tells us in 2 Corinthians 1:3-5. BUT.... He is not the God of the comfortable!!! Jesus had no place to lay His head. He worked tirelessly night and day and worked Himself to the point that He could sleep during what was probably like a monsoon. As a Christian, who is committed to living for Christ and being like Christ, it isn't about us being comfortable. We are meant to put ourselves in uncomfortable situations, to push ourselves, lay ourselves out there, pour ourselves out, give beyond what we think is possible. We are called to be living sacrifices, holy and pleasing to God (Rom. 12:1).

It is not what you say, it is what you do. Don't talk about it; be about it. Transformation happens in the action. We can pray and talk and dream and plan but until we take action, there are no wings, no wind, and no momentum.

Don't say, "I'm trying!" My friend was a boxer and said his dad always taught him there is no trying; there is only doing. He said, "Don't be a try baby." For you too, "Don't be a try baby!" "I'll try" is one of those phrases that fire me up whenever I hear someone say it. Instead you should say, "I will, I can, I am working on it, and I have done it." For those of you that profess Christ as Lord, when you say "I am," you are walking in the footsteps of the great I AM. There was no try with God; it was always I AM. Let your life be an example of the great I AM.

1. SET UP FOR SUCCESS

You have to set yourself up for success. It doesn't just happen by osmosis. It isn't just handed to you on a silver platter. You have to go after it with such dogged determination that nothing will sway your focus; nothing will get in your way.

In other parts of the book, I talked about the specific actions I took in order to set myself up for success in every area of my life. It will take time to invest in and figure out how to accomplish this for you.

Here is a brief overview of what you need to do to work through this:

1) Make affirmation-afformation-prayer sheet, set goals, set in present tense.
2) When will it occur?
3) Do a Core Value worksheet to develop values.
4) Be clear on the values you have.
5) What is it you stand for? There is an old saying that if you don't stand for something, you will fall for anything.
6) What is your mission statement for your personal life and what is your mission statement for your company or business?
7) What is your Vision? You must be very clear about your vision of where you are going.
8) Laminate your vision, goals and values. Put it where you can read it every day.

9) Start building your library now! Read, read, read. Study what you are trying to accomplish or overcome. You will be a 100% different person if you commit to reading books.
10) Listen to motivational clips every day like Jim Rohn or Anthony Robbins.
11) Listen to music that motivates you. When doing your Bible studies, listen to songs that make you sing and praise God. When working on your business, listen to songs that fire you up.

Repetition breeds mastery – it is the mother of all skills. Doing the same thing over and over and over and over again works. This will work whether you are working on something in your character or whether you are working on something in your life. What would happen if you worked every day on one of the things that you wanted to change every day? You will develop a skill set.

Success in becoming a better you and better at what you do is the discipline and dedication you put towards it. Most people aren't willing to do the things they need to do to make the change. You have to make the choice to make the change.

Knute Rockne, the famous Notre Dame football coach, used to say, "Drill, Drill, Drill" (Bettger, 2009). Die on the treadmill, nothing will get in the way of where you are going. You have to have the mentality that you will do whatever it takes. You have to make a commitment to be certain that at all costs you are going to do whatever it takes to change your life. It's all about committing. Whether it is entrepreneurship, a change in marriage, overcoming addiction, it is being willing to live a few years of your life like most people won't, so you can live the rest of your life like most people can't.

Spiritually, you have to set yourself up for success. Imagine that every day the devil plants seeds of doubt, fear or insecurity in you, the garden of your heart. I have to weed the garden every day to pull out the things he is trying to plant in me. I may have to take a tiller and till up the garden to make sure all of the weeds get pulled out from the root system. I must make sure the seeds are taken care of that have been planted: the seeds of righteousness, purity, truth, goodness, faithfulness. I have to water the seeds, give them a chance to grow, so I can eventually reap a harvest. If I don't pay attention to the garden or let the weeds grow up, they will choke out the seeds and I will not reap a harvest. My job is to care for my garden, to protect what is being planted in my heart, as well as take out the weeds. This will set me up for success.

In order to accomplish what we have been talking about, you have to start with your schedule. How and where are you spending your time? You must discipline yourself to spend your time on each of the areas that are important to you. Where you are going to INVEST your time? Keep in mind; you will reap what you sow, so where you invest is where you reap a harvest.

Here is an example of my daily calendar, which will give you an idea for how to set up a plan for yourself and how to discipline your time. The more specific you are the more you will accomplish whatever it is you set out to accomplish.

<u>My Perfect Day - Rituals and Habits</u>

4:00am – Get Up, Read/Study Bible

5:00am – Get on treadmill, Pray through Prayer List

6:00am – Get Boys Up, Make Protein Shake, Read Business Book, Get Ready

7:00am – Writing time for new book

8:00am – Agent Coaching/Training

9:00am – Prospecting!

12:00pm – Lunch - Check emails, return calls, negotiations

1:00pm – Listing Appointment OR Prospecting

3:00pm – Listing Appointment OR Prospecting

5:00pm – Make Dinner, Spend time talking with boys

6:00pm - Return Calls, Finish up Work

7:00pm – Family Time or Study Bible with women

9:00pm – Review Day, Goals, Pray, Go to Sleep

2. JUST DO IT

"Even if you are on the right track, you'll get run over if you just sit there." – Will Rogers

"Good is the enemy of great." – Jim Collins

"Time is our most valuable asset, yet we tend to waste it, kill it, and spend it rather than invest it." – Jim Rohn

As Nike so poignantly phrased it, JUST DO IT! It doesn't matter how much knowledge you have, how many degrees you have earned or how many opportunities you have been given. It all comes down to doing something about what you are aiming for.

When I first started coaching, I was told something that made my mind shift and got me going. My coach said it is like shooting a gun; you have ready, aim, fire. He said getting ready doesn't get the job done, aiming doesn't get it done, and you have to fire, fire again, fire, fire and fire again until you hit something. Eventually you will hit something. It may not be what you aimed at, but it is going to get you a lot closer if you just fire. I was so busy getting ready or aiming that before I fired I would hesitate. Many of the things we have talked about in the previous chapters are why I didn't fire and it took making a decision that no matter what the cost, no matter the humiliation, no matter if people screamed at me, didn't like me, slammed the door in my face, hung up on me, I had to keep firing. Fire, fire, fire,

fire.
It wasn't long until I hit something and, boy, did I hit something. I wound up getting an appointment with someone for a $500,000 listing, which I got. Then he had me list his wife's old house, which was $300,000 and I also sold, so that was another $300,000. Then when I had their house listed, I went around the neighborhood and received three other listings from that one house and they totaled $1,000,000 in listings, which I sold. Just from me saying over and over and over in my head, "Fire, fire, fire, fire, fire." I didn't back down, there was no going back and no retreating. I was all in to win and the efforts of my work were blessed.

I want to share a story that has changed my life. My coach, Hoss Pratt, shared this in a real estate training program. I think about this story when things come up where I'm faced with a battle in my life. It has had a big impact on my life. The story is called "Burn the Boats" (Andrews, 2007).

In February 1519, Hernando Cortez set sail on the final leg of a voyage that was to take him from Cuba, a stopover, to the shores of the Yucatán. He commanded 11 ships, with more than 500 soldiers, 100 sailors and 16 horses, bound for Mexico to take the world's richest treasure. The precious jewels, gold, silver, and sculptures sheltered on this limestone peninsula had been hoarded by the same army for over 600 years.

Everybody knew about this treasure because army after army tried to steal this treasure before. Army after army went in and failed. Now Cortez knew he had to have a different approach. Obviously Cortez was a smart guy, he knew that he had to change his approach. If army after army failed, he wasn't going in there and trying to fight like everybody else had.

Cortez knew his approach; he knew he had to have an army of people whose commitment was beyond that which the average person considered a commitment. Rather than just sign people up, Cortez laid out their vision. He laid out their vision for them. He told them what their lives would be like and how they would grow in wealth and favor. He found the best men and they sail. Now, halfway through the voyage, he realized that these men who were so certain before were starting to have doubts. These men were turning into whiners saying, "Mr. Cortez, please turn the ship around." They started having second thoughts. When they got to the island, they pulled their ships up. They didn't go in and conquer but waited on the beach. They waited on the beach and he gathered everyone around. He had talks about what their lives were going to be like. He talked about how their children were going to grow up and how they were going to grow up different than them. He painted a picture. These men were reminded of why they signed up.

The day came that they were going to go and take this treasure. It came and Cortez didn't go in and start fighting. He gathered the men together to have a talk and said three words that would change everything. As they listened, Cortez leaned in and said three simple words that changed everything: "Burn the boats." And they did, they burned the boats, they torched their own boats. Why? Because they had no choice but to win. They burned plan B. They burned their own boats. They went in and took the treasure. They won. They took the treasure that had been held by the same army for over 600 years. Why? They had no choice.

So my question to you is, "What are your boats? What's stopping you?" Get rid of your boats. Get rid of plan B. Go out there and be all in. Be committed. Just like Cortez and his army were. Be committed to change. Be committed to follow the exact action plan you determine to go from where you are now to where you want to be. Be committed to say affirmations. Be all in. No one will tell you no. You own it. You control your destiny. No one else does except God. Overcome your fears. Be all in. Define who you are.

The same thing works in your relationship with God. I was determined to take my relationship with Him to a different level. I did not want to be controlled by my feelings, to be dragged away and enticed by my fear, worry, doubt and insecurity. I had to be radical. I had to do something to show God I was serious and that I wasn't going to give in, that I wasn't going to let go until it changed.

If you remember, I mentioned a story where Jacob wrestled with the angel of God and said he wasn't going to let go until God blessed him. He didn't let go. He wound up with his hip socket taking a hit, but God blessed him because of his burning desire and persistence to not give up.

Being inspired by Hal Elrod (2014) in "The Miracle Morning," I made a decision that I was going to get up at 4 o'clock in the morning and I was going to spend the first 2 hours every morning with God. I determined that it was going to be me and God and we were going to wrestle in prayer and bible study until He blessed me and changed me. Luckily, I had been practicing Elrod's (2014) "The Miracle Morning" system for a few years, so I was used to disciplining myself. I tweaked the program so I could make sure the first two hours were devoted only to prayer and reading (Elrod, 2014). Then I had to be disciplined about using the next two hours to get all of the other things done, like reading to grow my business skills, journaling and writing.

I decided that I would read and pray from 4am-6am along with writing three things in my *Attitude of Gratitude* journal. I took my affirmations and put in all my prayers about each area of my life so that as I prayed, I was reading my affirmations and scriptures to support each one of them. During my prayer time, I visualized God answering my prayers and bringing about what I laid before Him.

Then at 6 a.m. I would get ready, get the boys off to school and spend time reading my business book. At 7 a.m. I started writing, which is when this book was written. After that I would be ready for my work day at 8 a.m.

I'm sure for many of you reading this, if you haven't read "The Miracle Morning" (Elrod, 2014), you are overwhelmed with just the thought of getting up at 4 a.m., but I can tell you that this has changed my life. I understand why Jesus got up while it was still dark to pray. There is a peace and a quietness that covers you like a blanket. It is the most amazing time of my entire day. Over time, I started waking up at three without an alarm. I would lie there and pray for God to let me sleep and let me rest until 4 a.m. Sometimes He does and sometimes He has so many things running through my brain that I have to get up and write it down. Most of the time it is something He has put in my mind, my dreams and my heart like what I put in this book.

After doing this for a few years, I received many benefits of having this discipline in my life. While this schedule was making a huge difference in me getting to my goal of having the closest relationship with God I could, I was inspired to go the extra mile and put in the extra effort. I made a decision I was going to go on a fast for at least two weeks so that I could have God answer some specific prayers I was laying before Him. I chose to do what is known as the *Daniel Fast*. For those of you who don't know the story, I wanted you to see why I chose this fast. Daniel 1:8-20 says:

> But Daniel made up his mind that he would not defile himself with the king's choice food or with the wine which he drank; so he sought permission from the commander of the officials that he might not defile himself. Now God granted Daniel favor and compassion in the sight of the commander of the

officials, and the commander of the officials said to Daniel, "I am afraid of my lord the king,
who has appointed your food and your drink; for why should he see your faces looking more haggard than the youths who are your own age? Then you would make me forfeit my head to the king." But Daniel said to the overseer whom the commander of the officials had appointed over Daniel, Hananiah, Mishael and Azariah, "Please test your servants for ten days, and let us be given some vegetables to eat and water to drink. "Then let our appearance be observed in your presence and the appearance of the youths who are eating the king's choice food; and deal with your servants according to what you see."

So he listened to them in this matter and tested them for ten days. At the end of ten days their appearance seemed better and they were fatter than all the youths who had been eating the king's choice food. So the overseer continued to withhold their choice food and the wine they were to drink, and kept giving them vegetables.

As for these four youths, God gave them knowledge and intelligence in every branch of literature and wisdom; Daniel even understood all kinds of visions and dreams.

Then at the end of the days which the king had specified for presenting them, the commander of the officials presented them before Nebuchadnezzar. The

> king talked with them, and out of them all not one was found like Daniel, Hananiah, Mishael and Azariah; so they entered the king's personal service. As for every matter of wisdom and understanding about which the king consulted them, he found them ten times better than all the magicians and conjurers who were in all his realm. (NASB)

We learn that Daniel made a decision about not eating meat from the king's table so that they would not be defiling God. God gave them knowledge, intelligence and wisdom and no one else was like them. They were ten times better in wisdom and understanding. Why in the world would I not want the same thing? I made a commitment to fast for two weeks for specific requests I wanted God to answer. The *Daniel Fast* is basically eating vegetables, fruits, beans and nuts. It is cutting out anything animal related, no meat, no fish or chicken and no dairy of any kind. I know that seems extreme, but when you show God you are serious about wanting Him to answer something and that you are willing to sacrifice in order to bring that about, you will be amazed at the outcome.

Daniel only drank water, since all they had back then was water or wine. When I made the decision to fast, it was put on my heart to give up coffee as well, even though coffee is a bean and grown from a plant. You have to realize that I was completely addicted to coffee. I made a decision to fast that as well. My thought in doing that was if I could fast from anything that is a struggle for me to give up then I could focus on purifying myself in every way for that time while focusing on God. At first, the thought of that was a little daunting since I could have been the official spokesperson for Starbucks. This was not going to be easy.

I'll tell you what really hit me about this topic. How ridiculous it was to me that I was struggling with giving up coffee to drink or certain foods that I loved, like cheese. Jesus gave up heaven, came to earth, lived in this fleshly tent, was persecuted, beaten, His skin ripped off of Him during the flogging, a two-inch crown of thorns beaten into His head, railroad steaks driven into His wrists and feet, crucified on a piece of wood, was pierced with a sword and died of a broken heart. He did that for me and I'm struggling with giving up coffee. Really??? Really??? He sacrificed everything for me and how can I not be willing to sacrifice coffee, donuts, or anything else in my life (worry, fear, sin) for Him. Do you see how ridiculous it is that we hold on to the things of this world or in our sinful nature instead of giving it all up for Him?

Anyways, back to the fast. What I found is that day-by-day, my focus started getting clearer, my body started feeling better and my mind started to open up. It was amazing how quickly the transformation started. I had people commenting on how beautiful my skin was and how clear it got. I noticed my pants were getting a little looser and, overall, I was feeling really good. God answered the prayers I put before Him during those two weeks. It was such an incredible experience that when the two-week time period was up, it was put on my heart to continue and follow in Daniel's example and allow God to transform me through my sacrifice. I decided I would continue with what I was doing and laying more out before God to see what He would do. He knew my heart was to sacrifice things that mattered to me so that I would show Him that I was serious about wanting things to change. Month after month, the miracles kept pouring in, the answered prayers kept coming. As I mentioned before, He had given me the ideas and words to write this book during that time, which I completed in 60 days. As well, my health continued to get better. Fat not only melted off of me, but all of the other baggage I carried around for so long like fear, worry, doubt and insecurity melted away. I am not saying I will eat this way forever, but at this point I have made a commitment to finish out this year and continue to see what miracles God will does.

You have to be willing to pay the price, willing to sacrifice, willing to go all in, give it 110%. There really is no other option if you want to have success. To the victor goes the spoils. You aren't going to become the victor by sitting on the couch. You aren't going to become a conqueror with your face in that gallon of ice cream. You have to take action!

For those of you stuck on my discussion of fasting and the change I made in my eating (because I know some of you are still rolling that thought around in your head), let me give you a little back up support with scriptures of why you need to take a really hard look at the way you eat.

Philippians 3:19 – "Their end is destruction, their god is

their belly, and they glory in their shame, with minds set on earthly things" (ESV).

Proverbs 23:20-21 – "Be not among drunkards or among gluttonous eaters of meat, for the drunkard and the glutton will come to poverty, and slumber will clothe them with rags."

Psalm 78:18 – "They tested God in their heart by demanding the food they craved."

1 Corinthians 6:19-20 – "Or do you not know that your body is a temple of the Holy Spirit within you, whom you have from God? You are not your own, for you were bought with a price. So glorify God in your body."

I believe this is one of the ways the devil is winning the battle in this world. He gets us comfortable, filling ourselves with everything that keeps us from being able to be transformed, because we are full of trash. I'm not one to get down on people. I like to keep my mind set on the positive things and on things above. There are times we have to wrestle with the devil and go against the dark forces of this world trying to win our souls. What I am going to share with you may be tough, but you need to dig deep to get out anything that gets in the way of your relationship with Him.

Let's think about this. You are crying out to God and crying to your friends about how miserable your life is; yet, you sit down and fill your body with everything known to man that was made to please your taste buds but kills the rest of your body. You are poisoning your body with the things you put in your mouth. You are putting chemicals you can't even pronounce, artificial everything and acid that erodes your esophagus. And you wonder why you don't have the motivation to do God's work or the mindset to be able to overcome anything.

God cares about what comes out of and what goes into your mouth. Are you honoring God with what goes into your mouth? Can you really be in a right relationship with Him if you are not examining every area of your life?

Some of you talk about how you are sober and how you have overcome your addictions, but God isn't blessing you as you take that puff off of your cigarette and blow smoke in God's face.

We are called to be holy and pleasing to God. You have to ask yourself, "What are you sacrificing?" Is it going to lunch a little later because you made it to church? What are you presenting to Him? What are you feeding Him? Your body becomes the temple of God, filled with His Holy Spirit at baptism. So your body really isn't even your own any more, you are borrowing it until the Day of Judgment. You are a guest in His house, in His dwelling place.

Here are a few scriptures about the body and what God thinks about it:

1 Corinthians 3:16-17 – "Don't you know that you

yourselves are God's temple and that God's Spirit dwells in your midst? If anyone destroys God's temple, God will destroy that person; for God's temple is sacred, and you together are that temple" (NIV).

Romans 12:1 – "Therefore, I urge you, brothers and sisters, in view of God's mercy, to offer your bodies as a living sacrifice, holy and pleasing to God— this is your true and proper worship."

1 Corinthians 6:20 – "You were bought at a price. Therefore honor God with your bodies."

2 Corinthians 4:10 – "We always carry around in our body the death of Jesus, so that the life of Jesus may also be revealed in our body."

1 Thessalonians 5:23 – "May God himself, the God of peace, sanctify you through and through. May your whole spirit, soul and body be kept blameless at the coming of our Lord Jesus Christ."

Philippians 3:17-19 – "Join together in following my example, brothers and sisters, and just as you have us as a model, keep your eyes on those who live as we do. For, as I have often told you before and now tell you again even with tears, many live as enemies of the cross of Christ. Their destiny is their destruction, their god is their stomach, and their glory is in their shame. Their mind is set on earthly things."

Matthew 26:41 – “Watch and pray so that you will not fall into temptation. The spirit is willing, but the body is weak.”
1 Corinthians 6:13 – “You say, ‘Food for the stomach and the stomach for food, and God will destroy them both.’ The body, however, is not meant for sexual immorality but for the Lord, and the Lord for the body.”

1 Peter 2:24 – "‘He himself bore our sins’ in his body on the cross, so that we might die to sins and live for righteousness; ‘by his wounds you have been healed.’"

Hebrews 10:10 – “And by that will, we have been made holy through the sacrifice of the body of Jesus Christ once for all.”

Deuteronomy 6:5 – “Love the Lord your God with all your heart, with all your soul, and with all your strength (body).”
Acts 2:38 – “Peter replied, ‘Repent and be baptized, every one of you, in the name of Jesus Christ for the forgiveness of your sins. And you will receive the gift of the Holy Spirit.’”

Jesus came in bodily form, so obviously the body is important to God. He offered His body for you. He gave it all up, laid it down. He was literally torn to pieces for you. His body was sacrificed and His blood was spilled. He used the body, which was broken, to bring us freedom, to give us hope.

I’m asking you to give it a chance, discipline your body for Him. Show Him you are thankful and grateful for His sacrifice by becoming a sacrifice yourself.

Putting bad food in our body doesn't allow our engine to run well. Our body is an engine. We have to fill our bodies with good things that will build us up, give us energy and provide us focus.

I am in no way saying you have to eat like I eat. What I am saying is if you really want the blessing of God, the love of God to be poured out on you like a barrel of water being poured over your head, you have to be willing to lay it all down and submit all of you to Him. For some of you it may be sacrificing food, for some sleep, for some coffee. He doesn't want left overs, He doesn't play second fiddle, He is a jealous lover and wants you all for Himself, no competition – not even yourself. He is in this to win it. You have to be too.

Realize that everything is a gift from God. Our body is a gift from God; it isn't ours so we need to take care of it. We are shepherds, overseers, representatives of these gifts, and we need to take care of each thing we are given because we are pleasing God and taking care of it. Our body, our children, our husbands, our pets, every single part of our lives is something He has handed us and asked us to take care of.

Like the parable of the talents, He is giving us the talents and wants us to use them, to multiply them, to use them to give back to Him when he visits us.

“Nothing is impossible, the word itself says I’m possible!”
– Audrey Hepburn

3. JARS OF CLAY

Let's begin with looking at when Jesus speaks with a Samaritan woman in John 4:4-42.

> Now he had to go through Samaria. So he came to a town in Samaria called Sychar, near the plot of ground Jacob had given to his son Joseph. Jacob's well was there, and Jesus, tired as he was from the journey, sat down by the well. It was about noon.
>
> When a Samaritan woman came to draw water, Jesus said to her, "Will you give me a drink?" (His disciples had gone into the town to buy food.)
>
> The Samaritan woman said to him, "You are a Jew and I am a Samaritan woman. How can you ask me for a drink?" (For Jews do not associate with Samaritans.)
>
> Jesus answered her, "If you knew the gift of God and who it is that asks you for a drink, you would have asked him and he would have given you living water."
>
> "Sir," the woman said, "you have nothing to draw with and the well is deep. Where can you get this living water? Are you greater than our father Jacob, who gave us the well and drank from it himself, as did also his sons and his livestock?"
>
> Jesus answered, "Everyone who drinks this water will be thirsty again, but whoever drinks the water I give

them will never thirst. Indeed, the water I give them will become in them a spring of water welling up to eternal life."

The woman said to him, "Sir, give me this water so that I won't get thirsty and have to keep coming here to draw water."

He told her, "Go, call your husband and come back."

"I have no husband," she replied.

Jesus said to her, "You are right when you say you have no husband. The fact is, you have had five husbands, and the man you now have is not your husband. What you have just said is quite true."

"Sir," the woman said, "I can see that you are a prophet. Our ancestors worshiped on this mountain, but you Jews claim that the place where we must worship is in Jerusalem."

"Woman," Jesus replied, "believe me, a time is coming when you will worship the Father neither on this mountain nor in Jerusalem. You Samaritans worship what you do not know; we worship what we do know, for salvation is from the Jews. Yet a time is coming and has now come when the true worshipers will worship the Father in the Spirit and in truth, for they are the kind of worshipers the Father seeks. God is spirit, and his worshipers must worship in the Spirit and in truth."

The woman said, "I know that Messiah" (called Christ) "is coming. When he comes, he will explain everything to us."

Then Jesus declared, "I, the one speaking to you—I am he."

Just then his disciples returned and were surprised to find him talking with a woman. But no one asked, "What do you want?" or "Why are you talking with her?"

Then, leaving her water jar, the woman went back to the town and said to the people, "Come, see a man who told me everything I ever did. Could this be the Messiah?" **30** They came out of the town and made their way toward him.

Meanwhile his disciples urged him, "Rabbi, eat something."

But he said to them, "I have food to eat that you know nothing about."

Then his disciples said to each other, "Could someone have brought him food?"

> "My food," said Jesus, "is to do the will of him who sent me and to finish his work. Don't you have a saying, 'It's still four months until harvest'? I tell you, open your eyes and look at the fields! They are ripe for harvest. Even now the one who reaps draws a wage and harvests a crop for eternal life, so that the sower and the reaper may be glad together. Thus the saying 'One sows and another reaps' is true. I sent you to reap what you have not worked for. Others have done the hard work, and you have reaped the benefits of their labor."
>
> Many of the Samaritans from that town believed in him because of the woman's testimony, "He told me everything I ever did." So when the Samaritans came to him, they urged him to stay with them, and he stayed two days. And because of his words many more became believers.
>
> They said to the woman, "We no longer believe just because of what you said; now we have heard for ourselves, and we know that this man really is the Savior of the world."

There are a few scriptures I would like to share with you to make this point.

The NIV version of 2 Corinthians 4:7 says: "But we have this treasure in jars of clay to show that this all-surpassing power is from God and not from us."

In the NLT, it states: "We now have this light shining in our hearts, but we ourselves are like fragile clay jar containing this great treasure. This makes it clear that our great power is from God, not from ourselves" (2 Cor. 4:7).

Have you ever been to a pottery class? It is so fascinating to watch them take a lump of clay that looks like a big blob. It is a big mass of nothing that is a formless, useless, colorless gray matter. Then they start to spin it. Using their hands, they mold it – slowly turning it, slowly shaping it.

God has done and is doing that to us. We were that blob. Maybe we let other people shape us instead of God. Maybe the shape that we are in at this point in our lives is pretty ugly. Maybe we don't even want to look at ourselves.

Now, imagine a jar of clay like the ones women used to carry to the well to gather their water each day. They would carry it on their shoulder and everyone could see it. They bring it to the well empty, set it on the ground and slowly lower it into the well that gives water, that gives life.

We have to empty ourselves. We have to get rid of the negative thoughts, insecurity, whatever sin you have. You need to be totally empty. When coming before God, I want to empty myself. I want to pour out what is in my jar, the trash that contaminates me.

Now that we have been formed and molded, we are used to carry life-giving water, useful for many purposes. However, first we have to allow God to mold us into the vessel that is best suited for the task He has for us to complete. Then we have to make sure we are not putting anything impure into our jar so that it doesn't contaminate the water. When we go to the well, just like the woman at the well, we will be filled up.

God wants to fill you up. He wants to give you living water. He wants to give you good things, but He can't if you haven't taken out the trash and rid yourself of the bad that is already filling you up. Imagine filling an Easter basket with all of the goodies you give your kids. You give them little toys, candy, cards, etc. God wants to fill you up with His goodies: love, joy, peace, patience, kindness, goodness and self-control. He wants you to be overflowing, spilling over the brim. He wants to make sure nothing else can get in the jar. He doesn't want impurities to get in there. You have to make sure none get in either. If one clump of dirt or one bottle of wine falls into the jar, they spread throughout the whole jar, making everything that was already in the jar spoiled, tainted, undrinkable and useless.

Our job is to protect the jar and what is in the jar. We have to cover the top, watch out for who is trying to take from the jar and make sure no one else is putting anything in the jar.

Throughout the day, we will take water out of the jar, serving here and giving there. We will use it to make food for our families, help out our neighbor. So we have been using what was given to us to give to others. At the end of the day we can know we did good with what we were given. Then, we have to go to the well again in the morning to fill up our jar and repeat it the next day. We can't skip a day. We need living water every day. We will be parched, thirsty, desperate and desolate without the water. We have to come the next morning and fill up again with His goodness. I hear people talk about not spending time with God in prayer and Bible study and then they wonder why their lives aren't going the way they want them to, they wonder why they aren't having victory in their lives. I see people gorging themselves with food but they won't gorge themselves with the Word and prayer. Don't try to go through the day without setting aside the time in the morning to prepare your heart and mind to connect with God and be energized with His Spirit to lead you through the day. Don't be surprised if the enemy tears you to shreds because he was up early preparing for you and very excited when you walked out of the house without your armor on.

After we have been filled with His goodies and His goodness, we can go about our day serving and giving and taking care of the needs of our families and people around us.

We have to empty ourselves. We have to get rid of the negative thoughts, insecurity, whatever sin you have. You need to be totally empty. I want to empty myself and pour out what is in my jar, take out the trash. Then I can be formed and molded.

We empty ourselves so that He can fill us up, sift us like

wheat, get rid of anything in us that isn't good, get rid of pride, selfishness and the like. We have to be sifted, to be cleansed, and to be purified. Only then, when we are empty, when we have nothing and are nothing, are open to letting Him fill us up, recognizing that He is the only one who can and will fill us up.

Stop trying to fill up with other things. That is like filling a car with bad gas. It will make the engine sputter or lock the engine up. It will ruin the car; destroy it. Same with filling ourselves up with things other than God. When He fills us up, the engine is a high performing engine, runs smooth, no noise, and purrs like a kitten. God wants to fill us up, but we have to be willing to empty ourselves. He doesn't make us do it. Like someone who is in love, they don't make someone marry them. We want the other person to love us and marry us because they love us. God is the same way, He wants us to love Him and be with Him because we want to, not because we have to.

Hopefully the visual of the jar helps you understand that we can be filled with His goodies, overflowing with all of the glory of heaven.

My daily prayer is that God will take out any trash in me that will get in the way of Him being able to fill me up. I want Him to pull out the weeds in the garden of my heart, so that the good seed can take root and create a harvest. When I start my prayer time, I pray for God to mold me, to make me into a mini-me, a representation and radiance of Christ. I pray for Him to forgive me for the sins I know I committed or struggled with the day before and to expose any sin I am not in touch with. I pray He exposes the desires of my heart so that I am not deceived and dragged away or enticed, so that I'm not taken off guard.

I will pray and imagine laying my mind, my mouth, my eyes, my heart, my hands, my feet, my body on the altar and that I'm giving every part of me to Him, to cleanse and purify so that when He gives it back to me, I will use it for His purposes.

I pray that because of Matthew 21:44, which says, "Anyone who falls on this stone will be broken to pieces; anyone on whom it falls will be crushed," as well as Matthew 23:12, "For those who exalt themselves will be humbled, and those who humble themselves will be exalted" (NIV). I want to choose to humble myself and lay all of my broken pieces before Him so He can put me back together in a way that will honor Him. I would prefer for Him to not to have to crush and humble me because I am arrogant or prideful. I would rather just go ahead and lay it all before Him and humble myself.

I pray He fills me back up with His Holy Spirit, He pours into me His living water, all the goodies – love, joy, peace, patience, kindness, gentleness and self control. I pray He will stuff me, fill me to the brim, overflowing. Then I pray He will give me someone else I can offer a drink of living water to.

To whom much is given, much is expected (Luke 12:48). I believe this also goes for those who have gone through a lot. We need to share to help others going through the same thing!

4. BECOMING A GO-GIVER

"The purpose of life is not to be happy. It is to be useful, to be honorable, to be compassionate, to have it make some difference that you have lived and lived well." – Ralph Waldo Emerson

In Acts 20:35, "The Lord Jesus himself said, 'It is more blessed to give than to receive.'"

There is a very small and powerful book called "The Go-Giver: A Little Story About a Powerful Business Idea" by Bob Burg and John David Mann (2007), which I highly recommend. It is a story of the journey of a changed life for someone who is seeking wealth, honor and fame (Burg & Mann, 2007). It is an interesting twist of events as it takes you through multiple encounters with people that ultimately helped enlighten the main character and predominately deals a lot with the character of a person and what motivates him (Burg & Mann, 2007). It is an interesting and quick read since the book is very short.

At the heart of the book is that you can't become what you want until you change who you are (Burg & Mann, 2007). This is true for us in real life as well. You won't be able to change your circumstances or change your life until you are willing to change who you are to become and who you want to be.

I have talked throughout this book about all of the things that God has offered to you. We need to be transformed into go-givers in order to truly have success in our lives. If you are still struggling with how to get there, how to overcome your mindset or your past consequences, there is still hope. In the beginning of the book, I told you that you were being handed the ability to have true success. God has his arms open wide waiting to give it to you, but I never told you exactly what it was. Before I do, I want to tell you a story.

I want you to go on a trip with me. If you have never been in love, this may be a little hard to imagine, but I want you to attempt to envision yourself in this situation. I want you to see yourself in a field, so wide and far that you can't see where it ends. You are standing in the middle of this field and there are tall blades of wheat so tall they almost come to your chest. The wheat is blowing in the wind and it is a warm summer day. You take in a breath of the fresh air, close your eyes and tilt your head up so you can feel the sun warming your face as it covers you like a blanket. You hear the voice of your love calling you and telling you they have a surprise for you. You decide you want it to really be a surprise so you put a blindfold over your eyes so you cannot see what they are talking about. They tell you they are going to take your hand and lead you to where they want you to go. You stumble as you are walking through the field. Even though you know there is nothing there, since you couldn't see anything else except miles and miles of fields and wheat, you are still struggling as your love leads you by the hand.

After what seems to be an eternity, you start to get

frustrated, not sure why you decided to put on the blindfold, frustrated that it is taking so long. But you have a basket in one hand and don't want to let go of your loves hand, so you decide to leave the blindfold on. You are having a hard time walking, tripping on the rocks and sticks on the ground, stumbling over things you can't really tell what they are, and you have had enough. You tell your love to stop because you are taking off the blindfold. Once you do, you take hold of your loves hand and you start running through the fields. Nothing is stopping you, nothing is tripping you up. You are working together in unison, running and laughing together. You can't believe it took you so long to stop and take off the blind fold. You are irritated with yourself, but you are so overcome with the love you feel inside for your love that you quickly forget about the blind fold and soak in the overwhelming sensation of true love.

This is what our relationship with God is like. He is our love, wanting to lead us to a surprise. He didn't put the blindfold on us, we did. Our sins and struggles are our blindfold. It keeps us from seeing where we are going. It trips us up and makes us stumble along the way. It keeps us from enjoying our love and running towards the surprise waiting for us.

God's love is the greatest gift and where we find true success. In 1 John 4:8, it says, "Whoever does not love does not know God, because God is love." It is because of His love that I can overcome my past. It is because of His love that I can have victory over my character flaws. It is because of His love that I can have a sound mind and overcome mental illness. It is because of His love that I don't have to allow my body to be used by men. It is His love that is the cure for my insecurity. That is why He said there is no fear in love. When we are really in His love, we are running happy and free, completely lost in His love. We aren't consumed with fear and doubt because we are so overtaken by His love that it washes all of those things away. When we are so in love with Him and so consumed by His love, we aren't focusing on getting things from other people or things in this world. We are confident because we know He will take care of us and provide for us because we know His love so intensely.

1 John 4:18 – "There is no fear in love. But perfect love drives out fear, because fear has to do with punishment. The one who fears is not made perfect in love."

This is a perfect scripture to describe what it all comes down to. If we come to understand and grasp His love, there is no fear, there are no worries, no doubts, no struggles. Just like the story about running through the fields with your love, there is nothing else that concerns you, nothing that is holding you back. You are all in, completely committed, giving yourself over to that person. When we are like that, there is no fear. That is what God wants for you. He wants you to grab hold of that love and be so overcome by it that it drives out everything else, fills you up to overflowing and enables you to overcome any struggle. You are willing to give anything up to keep that love because there is truly nothing else that compares to it.

I want God to be my CEO. I want Him to be my master and my owner. I gladly surrender my will to Him and submit to His authority. He is the perfect leader, perfect Father and owns everything so He has all of the money to bless me in any way He so desires. He is the one with all of the knowledge, understanding, power and majesty. Everything is His and there is nothing hidden from His sight. That is who I want to follow. That is who I can trust.

1 John 4:16 – "This is love: not that we loved God, but that he loved us and sent his Son as an atoning sacrifice for sins" (NLT).

Romans 8:32 – "He who did not spare His own Son, but gave him up for us all – how will he not also, along with him, graciously give us all things?" (ESV).

Did you get that? Even if you haven't had a relationship with Him and loved Him, he has already demonstrated His love for you. He has already given up His Son as a sacrifice for you. He watched His Son be tortured, flogged, crucified and murdered for you. He has already done the work for you to be able to be forgiven. You just need to respond to His love. You just need to reach out your hand and take your loves hand and let Him free you from all of the trials, temptations and situations you are going through. What the devil uses to enslave you, God intends to use to free you. You just need to get out of the trash pile and come to the party!

Romans 8:38-39 – "For I am convinced that neither death

nor life, neither angels nor demons, neither the present nor the future, nor any powers, neither height nor depth, nor anything else in all creation, will be able to separate us from the love of God that is in Christ Jesus our Lord" (NIV).

I imagine that I'm a little girl hanging onto her daddy's leg as he walks around the house. I won't let go; I will hang on for dear life, since I know I am in for the ride of my life. Then my perfect Daddy bends down and picks me up in His arms and wraps His arms around me, letting me know I am safe and protected and that He will always take care of me.

There is a song I think of when I think of God's love. Part of the song I skip, since it is talking about a man's love for a woman, but much of the song perfectly describes how I feel about God.

Before I give you the lyrics to the song, there are two scriptures that help paint the picture of the story I just told and the song I am getting ready to share with you.

Isaiah 41:10b – "I will strengthen you and help you; I will uphold you with my righteous right hand."

Isaiah 41:13 – "For I am the Lord your God who takes hold of your right hand and says to you, Do not fear; I will help you."

Here are the words to a portion of the song:

"It's Your Love" by Stephony Smith

Oh, it's a beautiful thing
Don't think I can keep it all in
I've just gotta let you know
What it is that won't let me go

It's your love
It just does something to me
It sends a shock right through me
I can't get enough
And if you wonder
About the spell I'm under

Oh it's your love
Better than I was
More than I am
And all of this happened
By taking your hand
And who I am now
Is who I wanted to be
And now that we're together
I'm stronger than ever, I'm happy and free

Oh, it's a beautiful thing
Don't think I can keep it all in
And if you ask me why I've changed
All I gotta do is say your sweet name

It's your love
It just something to me

It sends a shock right through me

I can't get enough
And if you wonder
About the spell I'm under
Oh it's your love (Smith, 1997, Everywhere)

God wants to run through the fields with you, holding your hand, showing you all of the wonders of His creation. He wants to lavish His love on you and pour out His favor on your life.

What an honor to love and be loved by God. What an honor to be used by Him to do His good works. What an honor that I get to be transformed into a new creation here on earth and then again in heaven. What an honor that I get to know Him and be known by Him both intimately and completely. What a privilege to be called a daughter of God. What a blessing to be a princess and have a Father who is King. God is my precious reward, my Lord, my strength, my shield. He is my protector. He goes before me and stands behind me. He wraps Himself around me and fills me with His Spirit.

As Albert Einstein said, "Happiness is the key to success." True success comes not from having things but from bringing every part of your life into complete unity and being filled with the unconditional love of God, as well as pouring out that love to others with nothing standing in your way.

Now that you have the hope of the gift and now that you have the plan of how to attack every area of your life, to overcome the obstacles that have gotten in the way to your success, now is the time to make the change. Now is the time to burn the boats.

Once you have conquered your fears, changed your life, created the dream, you must think about how to give back, how to pay it forward, how to return the favor, how to become a go-giver.

This book has been my go-giver. It is my way to pour into someone everything that has been given to me. I hope and pray this book has been a blessing to you. I hope that after reading it, you are never the same.

With His Love,

Sheila Fejeran

5. MY PRAYER

I pray for your heart and mind to be open to everything you have read in this book. I pray that you will be encouraged, inspired and committed to changing your relationship with God. I pray that you will be willing and desperate enough to do whatever it takes to change anything in your life that gets in the way of drawing closer to Him. That you will create the life that you have always desired and that He has always planned for you.

I pray that once you do, you will know and feel the overwhelming love of God in your life and that you will be renewed and transformed into the likeness of His Son, Jesus Christ. All for His glory and honor and praise!

I pray also that God will circle this nation. This was founded as "One Nation Under God." This prayer is for us to be known again as His nation and His people. I pray that God will take hold of us. I pray that God will raise up a remnant. That we will circle the walls, that we will get on our knees and raise our hearts and our eyes and our hands towards heaven. God I know that You are our King, You alone are our Lord, our Savior and our Hope. God, You have set aside those whose hearts are Yours. You are the one who will save us from the enemy. You have already saved us and You have already conquered. You have already won the battle. We just need to take hold of it. We need to rise up, we need to go to battle, the way You parted the sea and saved a nation from an army. The way You used 3,000 to conquer an army and You chose those that lapped the water instead of using their hands. Father, You love the impossible odds, You love the overwhelming situations, You love when we realize there is no way possible for us to do it. That is when You are glorified, that is when You show Yourself, that is when we see Your glory, when we know there is no other way. You rain down quail in the desert, You do the impossible, and You are the great I AM. You are wanting and waiting for us to call out, to give it to You, to be desperate, to beg for help, to surrender our pride and our agenda.

Father, I lay before You the hearts of every person's eyes that are reading this book, that You will open the eyes of their heart, that You will get between them and their circumstances, that You will go before them and fight their battles. I pray, Lord, that You will change their lives, so that they can know You, know Your incomprehensible love, and know Your kindness, tolerance and patience. And Father, I pray more than anything else that once they are changed that they will say "thank you" with their lives for all You have done for them.

I pray all of this in Your son, Jesus Christ's, precious name. Amen – So be it!

REFERENCES

Allen, David. (2003). *Getting Things Done: The Art of Stress-Free Productivity*. London, England: Penguin Books.

"Amazon Review: Hal Elrod's 'The Miracle Morning.'" (n.d.). *Amazon*. Retrieved from http://www.amazon.com/Miracle-Morning-Not-So-Obvious-Guaranteed Transform/dp/0979019710.

Andrews, Andy. (2007). Burn the Boats. Retrieved from https://www.andyandrews.com/eblast/051507.html.

Attitude. (n.d.). *Google.* Retrieved on April 27, 2016, from https://www.google.com/?gws_rd=ssl#q= attitude+definition.

Autosuggestion. (n.d.). *Oxford Dictionaries.* Retrieved on April 27, 2016, from http://www.oxforddictionaries.com/us/definition/american_english/ autosuggestion.

Batterson, Mark. (2014). *The Grave Robber: How Jesus Can Make Your Impossible Possible.* Grand Rapids, MI: BakerBooks.

Bettger, Frank. (2009). *How I Raised Myself from Failure to Success in Selling.* New York, NY: Prentice Hall Press.

Blood Cell Formation. (2016). *Encyclopedia Britannica.*

Retrieved from http://www.britannica .com /science/blood-cell-formation.

Blood Vessels. (2016). *The Franklin Institute.* Retrieved from https://www.fi.edu/heart/blood-vessels.

Burg, Bob & Mann, John David. (2007). *The Go-Giver: A Little Story About a Powerful Business Idea.* London, England: Penguin Books, Ltd.

Desire. (n.d.). *Google*. Retrieved on April 27, 2016, from https://www.google.com/?gws_rd=ssl#q=desire.

Desperate. (n.d.). *Google*. Retrieved on April 27, 2016, from https://www.google.com/webhp sourceid= chrome-instant&ion=1&espv=2&ie=UTF 8#q=definition%20desperate.

Elrod, Hal. (2014). *The Miracle Morning: The Not-So Obvious Secret Guaranteed to Transform Your Life*. Hal Elrod International, Inc.

Faith. (n.d.). *Dictionary.com.* Retrieved on April 27, 2016, from http://www.dictionary.com/browse/faith.

Farb, Peter. (1993). *Word Play: What Happens When People Talk.* New York, NY: Vintage Books.

Focus. (n.d.). *Dictionary.com.* Retrieved on April 27, 2016, from https://www.google.com /webhp?sourceid =chrome-instant&ion=1&espv=2&ie=UTF-8#q=

definition%20focus.

Gibbs, Laura. (2002). *Aesop's Fables: A New Translation By Laura Gibbs*. Oxford, fable
237.

Gladwell, Malcolm. (2008). *Outliers: The Story of Success*. New York, NY: Little, Brown and Company.

Hill, Napoleon. (2000). *Think and Grow Rich*. Meriden, CT: The Ralston Society.

I Am: The Film. (2011). Retrieved from http://www.iamthedoc.com/thefilm

Inspirational Quotes: Maxwell Maltz. (n.d.). *En-Theos*. Retrieved on April 27, 2016 from

https://www.entheos.com/quotes/by_teacher/maxwell+maltz.

Intent. (n.d.). *Dictionary.com.* Retrieved on April 27, 2016, from http://www.dictionary.com /browse/intent.

Jeary, Tony. (2009). *Strategic Acceleration: Succeed at the Speed of Life*. Danvers, MA: Vanguard Press.

Kiyosaki, Robert. T. & Trump, Donald. (2013). *Why We Want You to Be Rich: Two Men – One Message*. Scottsdale, AZ: Plata Publishing, LLC.

Kling, Tammy. (2014, January 24). Words are Currency [Web log post]. Retrieved from http://www.tammykling.com/words-are-currency/.

Lockridge, S.M. (1976). That's My King. Retrieved from http://across2u.com/ThatsMyKing.html.

Luske, H.S, & Sharpsteen, B. (Directors). Disney, W. (Produces, & Sears, T., Cottrell, W., Penner, E., & Battaglia, A. (Writers). 1940. *Pinocchio* [Motion picture]. United States: RKO Radio Pictures.

Maltz, Maxwell. (1960). *Psycho-Cybernetics*. New York, NY: Prentice-Hall, Inc.

Martin. Gary. (2012). *The Phrase Finder: Sticks and stones may break my bones.* Retrieved September 22, 2012.

Marvanne, Rhema. (2011). Just as I Am [Recorded by Marvanne, R.]. On *Believe* [CD]. Rhema Productions Inc.

Mindset. (n.d.). *Google*. Retrieved on April 27, 2016, from https://www.google.com/?gws_rd=ssl#q= mindset+definition.

Nightingale, Earl. (2006). *The Strangest Secret*. Grand Rapids, MI: BN Publishing.

Nose, Sinuses and Smell. (2016). *InnerBody.* Retrieved on April 27, 2016, from http://www.innerbody.com/anim/nasal.html.

Olson, Jeff. (2013). *The Slight Edge: Secret to a Successful Life*. Austin, TX: Greenleaf Book Group, LLC.

Smith, Stephony. (1997). It's Your Love [Recorded by Tim Mc.Graw. Featuring Faith Hill.] On *Everywhere* [CD]. Curb.

St. John, Noah. (2006). *The Great Little Book of Afformations*. Dracut, MA: MetaPublishing.

Steriade, M. (1996). "Arousal: Revisiting the Rectangular Activating System." *Science* **272** (5259): 225-226 doi:10.1126/science.272.5259.225.PMID 8602506

Tennyson (1854). *The Charge of the Light Brigade*. The Poetry Foundation. Retrieved on 04 April 2016 from http://www.poetryfoundation.org/poem/174586.

Visualization. (n.d.). *Merriam-Webster* online dictionary. Retrieved on April 27, 2016, from http://www. merriam-webster.com/dictionary/visualization.

Following are some of the affirmations I pray through every day. This is not a complete list, but enough for you to get an idea of how specific I am about my desires, my plans and the actions I need to take to make them happen. When you sit down to create yours, remember the more specific you can be the better. You want to dig out whatever is in your heart and lay out a plan for true success!

PRAYER LIST (AFFIRMATIONS – AFFORMATIONS)

Matthew 7:7-8 – "Ask and it will given to you; seek and you will find; knock and the door will be opened to you. For everyone who asks receives, the one who seeks finds; and to the one who knocks, the door will be opened."

Fill me with the mind of Christ, the desire of Christ and mold me and make me into a representative of Christ, the radiance of Christ.

Hebrews 1:3 – "The Son is the radiance of God's glory and the exact representation of his being, sustaining all things by his powerful word. After he had provided purification for sins, he sat down at the right hand of the Majesty in heaven."

Forgive me, sift me, take out all of the sinful nature, keep my sin before me (Psalm 51:3).

Open my eyes and heart, that I may have a raw, daily dependence on God.

Hebrews 4:13 – "Nothing in all creation is hidden from God's sight. Everything is uncovered and laid bare before the eyes of him to whom we must give account."

<u>GOD/SOUL</u> – I am committed to growing in my relationship with God, in faith, trust and gratitude.

<u>I Will Have Faith. Why is my faith sure and certain?</u>

Romans 10:17 – "Consequently, faith comes from hearing the message, and the message is heard through the word about Christ."

Hebrews 12:2 – "Fix your eyes on Jesus, the author and perfecter of our faith" (NKJV).

Hebrews 11:1 – "Now faith is confidence in what we hope for and assurance about what we do not see" (NIV).

Hebrews 11:6 – "And without faith it is impossible to please him, for whoever would draw near to God must believe that he exists and that he rewards those who seek him" (ESV).

Jesus is the one that gives me faith and the one that perfects my faith. I have to fix my eyes on Him, not on myself or what I have to do. I must keep working to focus on Him, imitate Him, serve Him so my faith with grow. Faith celebrates and thanks God for things before they happen.

It is all about what I focus on! Look UP and fix your eyes on Him.

<u>I Do Believe. Why do I have such secure belief?</u>

Mark 11:24 – "Therefore I tell you, whatever you ask in prayer, believe that you have received it, and it will be yours."

Mark 9:24 – "Immediately the boy's father exclaimed, "'I do believe; help me overcome my unbelief!'" (NIV).

Genesis 15:6 – "And he believed the LORD, and He counted it to him as righteousness." Be the one saying, "Here I am, Send Me!"

<u>I Will Trust God. Why do I have complete trust?</u>

Joshua 1:9 – "Have I not commanded you? Be strong and courageous. Do not be afraid; do not be discouraged, for the LORD your God will be with you wherever you go."

Psalm 9:1 – "Those who know your name trust in you, for you, LORD, have never forsaken those who seek you."

Proverbs 3:5-6 – "Trust in the LORD with all your heart and lean not on your own understanding; in all your ways submit to him, and he will make your paths straight."
I will trust in God, lean on His understanding and not my own, submit to Him in mind, thought, attitude and action, knowing He will make my paths straight.

I Will Be Grateful. Why do I have such an intense gratitude?

James 1:17 – “Every good and perfect gift is from above, coming down from the Father of the heavenly lights, who does not change like shifting shadows.”

Colossians 3:17 – “And whatever you do, whether in word or deed, do it all in the name of the Lord Jesus, giving thanks to God the Father through him.”

Romans 1:21 – “For although they knew God, they neither glorified him as God nor gave thanks to him, but their thinking became futile and their foolish hearts were darkened.”

I will focus on glorifying God, not myself, for who He is and thanking Him for what He has done and continues to do for me.

I Will Be Humble. Why am I so humble and broken?

Luke 14:11 – “For all those who exalt themselves will be humbled, and those who humble themselves will be exalted."

Matthew 21:44 – “Anyone who falls on this stone will be broken to pieces; anyone on whom it falls will be crushed."

I choose to humble myself before God, lay all my sin and needs before Him and let Him put me back together in a way that glorifies Him.

I Will Be a Living Sacrifice. Why am I so happy being a living sacrifice for God?

Romans 12:1 – "Therefore, I urge you, brothers and sisters, in view of God's mercy, to offer your bodies as a living sacrifice, holy and pleasing to God--this is your true and proper worship."

I am committed to making Jesus Christ Lord of my life. I will put Him first in my thoughts, attitudes and actions. I am committed to becoming a living sacrifice, an example of my devotion to Him. I will say "thank you" with my life.

HEALTH/BODY - My dream/goal is to keep in shape, to be at an optimal weight for my health. I am committed to love and care for my body.

Why do I have such a healthy body?

1 Corinthians 6:20 - "You were bought at a price. Therefore honor God with your bodies."

I will exercise by walking on the treadmill at least 1 hour, 4 days a week. I will do yoga/sit-ups/push-ups 2 days a week so that I can have the energy and focus I need to accomplish my goals.

I will think before I eat so what goes in my body will help me accomplish my goal of living healthy. I will eat fruits and vegetables, nuts and seeds. I will drink 64 oz. of water per day.

<u>**MIND**</u> – My dream/goal is to be fearless; to be secure and self-controlled with a sound mind.

<u>I Will Not Fear. Why is there no fear with God?</u>

1 John 4:18 – "There is no fear in love. But perfect love drives out fear, because fear has to do with punishment. The one who fears is not made perfect in love."

1 John 4:8 – "Whoever does not love does not know God, because God is love."

Matthew 17:20 – "He replied, 'Because you have so little faith. Truly I tell you, if you have faith as small as a mustard seed, you can say to this mountain, 'Move from here to there,' and it will move. Nothing will be impossible for you.'" *Speak to the mountain!*

We overcome fear through our faith in and love for God. God is love, in His perfect love He drives out fear. There is no fear in love.

Genesis 4:7 – "If you do what is right, will you not be accepted? But if you do not do what is right, sin is crouching at your door, it desires to have you, but you must master it."

I AM FEARLESS.

I will set my mind on things above. Why do I have my mind set on things above?

Romans 12:2 – "Do not conform any longer to the pattern of the world, but be transformed by the renewing of your mind."

Philippians 4:8 – "Finally, brothers and sisters, whatever is true, whatever is noble, whatever is right, whatever is pure, whatever is lovely, whatever is admirable – if anything is excellent or praiseworthy – think about such things."

I will have a sound mind & self-control. Why do I have such a sound mind and self-control?

2 Timothy 1:7 – "For the Spirit God gave us does not make us timid, but gives us power, love and self-discipline."

I control my thoughts. Why have I been so successful taking captive my thoughts?

2 Corinthians 10:5 – "We take captive every thought and make it obedient to Christ."

I will never talk negative. Why am I so encouraging when I speak to others?

1 Peter 4:11 – "If anyone speaks, they should do so as one who speaks the very words of God."

Matthew 12:36 – "I tell you, on the day of judgment people

will give account for every careless word they speak" (ESV).

Luke 6:45 – "For out of the overflow of the heart, the mouth speaks" (BSB).

OUR WORDS ARE X-RAYS OF OUR HEARTS

<u>I push myself beyond my quit factor every day. Why can I push myself so much?</u>

Philippians 4:13 – "I can do all things through Christ who strengthens me" (NKJV).

<u>I have a mindset of abundance, (not scarcity). Why have I been so abundantly blessed by God?</u>

Romans 8:28 – "…In all things God works for the good of those who love him, who have been called according to his purpose" (NIV).

<u>I will take responsibility for my choices. Why do I reap such amazing blessings?</u>

Galatians 6:7 – "Do not be deceived: God cannot be mocked. A man reaps what he sows."

Proverbs 28:13 – "Whoever conceals their sins does not prosper, but the one who confesses and renounces them finds mercy."

I reap what I sow. I will plant good seeds and pull the weeds up so I can reap a harvest in each area of my life.

"A man can fail many times, but he isn't a failure until he begins to blame somebody else." – John Burroughs

PERSONAL DEVELOPMENT

BURN THE BOATS – NO QUITTING, NO GOING BACK, NOW IS THE TIME – DO IT NOW!!!!

Work like it depends on me and pray BECAUSE it depends on God! Act AS IF He is going to answer your prayers.

My desire is that I will Live a life with such authentic integrity that those who know me best actually respect me most.

I HAVE A RESPONSIBILITY TO LIVE MY LIFE TO THE FULLEST AND ACHIEVE MY GOALS IN ORDER TO SET AN EXAMPLE FOR THOSE AROUND ME. In creating the life I want, I can't wait for someday or some year in the future. NOW is my time!

"The way you live your life gives everyone else around you permission to do the same." – Hal Elrod

"I choose to live in solutions, finding tools and opportunities to meet my goals."
– Unknown

“Simple Daily Disciplines – Your Philosophy Creates Your Actions, Attitudes, Results – Create Your Life.” – Jeff Olson

“Your level of success will seldom exceed your level of personal development because success is something you attract by the person you become.” – Jim Rohn

“You will never change your life until you change something you do daily. The secret to your success is found in your daily routine.” – John Maxwell

79965336R00098

Made in the USA
Columbia, SC
01 November 2017